The Six Hundred Press
Jackson, Mississippi
the-600.com

First Edition

THE SIX HUNDRED PRESS

The Centsable Startup
Tom Bunting

Table of Contents

Prologue

The following manuscript is a rewritten summation of my blog
sessions to which I engaged after my retirement from my startup
company, Common CENTS Solutions. It is a description of
Common CENTS Solutions' evolution, how it began and
developed into a viable force in the marketplaces it served.
It is also a synopsis of the philosophies and policies I deployed to
sustain a dynamic workplace and the archetype for exceptional
customer service.

I dedicate this volume to the many fine and dedicated
employees that helped establish and grow Common CENTS
Solutions into the multimillion-dollar business it matured
into by the time I retired.

So, You're Thinking About A Startup

Welcome to CENTSable Startup – Lessons learned in starting and building a software business organically.

This is not the story of a bold entrepreneur who risks it all on a new venture, but rather the narrative of a dedicated employee who acts on an idea to improve his company's performance and evolves it into a full-fledged independent business. Perhaps this storyline is a more sanguine profile of how a budding entrepreneur can exploit the possibilities of private enterprise with a safer, more secure approach.

My guess is there are countless concealed individuals working within corporations with hidden aspirations for launching their own businesses, but are restrained by financial obligations, family responsibilities or a general fear of losing the income and fringe benefit security that their current employment represents.

This book is devoted to the lessons learned, both positive measures taken as well as regretful decisions made, in developing a simple idea into a privately owned business eventually sold for a multi-million dollar sum. I will discuss all aspects of the evolutionary process as I experienced it, including topics of strategic planning, funding, branding, marketing, staffing, organizational structure, corporate culture, sales strategy, product development, product support, customer relations and more. Because the primary focus of our company was application software, much of the conversation will involve information technology, but the concepts apply to most any business type and will be relevant to all organizations.

Creating a startup company from within an existing organization may not exactly be "free" enterprise, but it is much less a financial gamble than taking the solo plunge and risking it all... especially when you consider the overwhelming failure rate of new companies.

Luck Is When Preparation Meets Opportunity

Starting a business actually begins long before the idea strikes you. It really begins with your job experiences leading up to the incubation environment. In my case it was the learned fundamental principles of:

· Distribution and accounts receivable in my very first job – a paper route at age 11;

· Branding, inventory, pricing and customer service in my part-time retail men's clothing jobs throughout high school and college;

· Production and labor basics from my factory work during college summer recesses;

· Information technology in my first true fulltime employment as a programmer trainee which later graduated to a systems analyst;

· Sales, marketing and management from my computer sales career with Fortune 500 companies, one of which was NCR (National Cash Register Co.).

All of which led me to my launching pad job with a contract foodservice management firm, where I took on the responsibilities of contract negotiations, budgeting, and information systems, working my way up the corporate ladder to Vice President on the company's management team.

But none of it happened just by chance. Each experience set the stage and prepared me for the next, primarily because I took each job or responsibility seriously with the earnest intent to learn and do my best at each. Which leads me to identify a few essential personal characteristics you must have to even contemplate running your own show:

1. Work ethic – the willingness to devote whatever effort is required to get a job done.

2. Intellectual curiosity – the motivation to investigate and delve into the mechanics of a task to gain understanding and expertise.

3. Moral judgment – the strength of character to always base decisions on "doing the right thing", never for expediency or personal gain.

These characteristics are paramount to being successful in any endeavor, because they serve as the foundation to building trust. Dependability, knowledge, and integrity, which these character traits represent, will attract attention and build confidence in an organization, whether they be customers, employees, vendors, peers or shareholders. Certainly, these vital characteristics will be referenced many more times throughout this book.

Then The Idea Strikes You

So here I am in the 1980's imparting my best efforts to benefit the enterprise for which I was employed when suddenly the inspiration dawned on me. For me it was relating the cash control principles I learned as a sales representative for the NCR (National Cash Register) Company with an ignored point-of-sale function in the hospital cafeterias managed by the Food Service Contractor for which I was then employed.

To provide a little background, hospitals at that time were still mostly operating as non-profits, naïve of much business acumen. And the government hadn't yet instituted the Medicare healthcare reforms that would transform runaway medical costs into today's more controllable form. For hospitals back then the business aspects of their retail operations were completely overlooked and any losses in the retail arena were simply recovered through increased patient charges the following year. Little wonder why healthcare ran excessive double-digit inflation in those years.

My background had educated me to the mistakes and abuses that can occur at point-of-sale registers and I saw an obvious connection with the lack of control in these healthcare organizations. This awareness naturally pointed to certain processes that are found in many facets of business.

· Identifying a need – even though the organization may be unaware of their neediness.

· Estimating results in solving the need – perhaps in better revenues, cost savings, productivity gains, customer service advances, etc.

· Justifying the pursuit of the solution – determining the investment and the anticipated return on the investment (ROI).

As I will explore in later chapters, these steps are key components as well in the sales process. I will explain how to conduct the sales survey to uncover customer needs and offer a sales proposition to justify their investment in the solution. But that will have to wait for now.

However, this inspiration also led to the biggest question of all. Do I develop this concept within my current employer's organization and therefore forfeit the rights to any outcome, or do I explore taking this idea and launching an independent venture, maintaining ownership in its creation. The answer depends on the market potential for the concept, the capacity to fund the project, the ability to supplement living costs until the finished product is revenue producing and any dealings with personal and/or family constraints.

For me at the time, glum personal finances and the security of a dependable paycheck discouraged a private venture and mandated I develop the idea within the confines of my employer. And this is not so unusual: you might remember that it was a 3M chemist who dreamed up Post It notes. And more recently on a popular television show, "Shark Tank", a bartender in partnership with his restaurant employer pitched his wine aeration idea to the show's investor panel. So, like these other *wantrepreneurs* I chose the path of cultivating my idea while remaining with my employer.

Hatching The Plan

With the first big decision behind me, to stay within the confines of the company, I could now focus on promoting my idea full on. To start I had to organize my approach before I could actually begin my promotion. This included several key steps:

1. Ascertain what components would be required to shape my idea.

2. Determine how my solution would be constructed.

3. Decide where a prototype might be implemented as a pilot.

The first of the steps had one obvious component – a cash register device. But it really wasn't that simple because there had to be longer term thinking regarding where the point-of-sale technology was headed, how any solution fit into the automation plans of the corporation, and what was practical to develop considering limited human and financial resources.

Although I envisioned a solution constructed on a back-office PC connected to a POS device, the reality of my budget called for a more prudent approach. My fallback position was to simply implement a lower cost, standalone cash register and let it serve as proof of concept. I trusted that the organization's POS control was so blatantly deficient, that even the most rudimentary system would show surprisingly positive results.

Deciding on a pilot site was much easier. My employer company, outside of Healthcare, also managed food services in the Educational and Industrial verticals and one Manufacturing customer's cafeteria was already under suspicion for underperforming cash receipts.

To make a long story short, in that Manufacturer's cafeteria we did implement an inexpensive electronic cash register with enough sophistication to apply the sought after controls and immediately cash receipts increased $1,000 a week. Needless to say, my proof of concept was an eye opener for my corporate executives and provided me an attentive audience for my expansive proposals to come.

The message here is that although my idea was much broader than what turned out as a pilot, compromises are often required. Taking smaller steps may be required before the big leap is possible. Having a scaled down model that facilitates acceptance to move forward, yet still demonstrates the value and justification of the bigger concept is a wise move.

Turning The Plan Into Action

With the promise of profits demonstrated by the point-of-sale pilot, I received authorization to hire two additional employees, 1 programmer and 1 installer, to implement the full program. We decided our application would be developed in the programming language of the day, COBOL, and operated under Microsoft's disk operating system (DOS) on a personal computer (PC). The application's purpose was:

1. Allow a cafeteria manager to set up a week's food selection menu in our English language, back office application and have it load instructions that the cash registers could interpret and execute.

2. Collect electronically the point-of-sale results from the registers and produce easily readable reports to assure sales were recorded, inventory accounted and cash balanced.

3. Monitor cashier activities to limit abuse and measure productivity.

Our first hurdle was to identify a point-of-sale device that could facilitate our priorities. We preferred to find an existing POS system rather than concoct our own for several practical reasons:

· Accelerate our development time by not reinventing the POS paradigm.

· Facilitate on-site maintenance of hardware devices through a network of authorized dealers.

· Reap the advantages of a third party's dedication to POS research, development and support.

We discovered a register system that we could adapt from Micros Systems, Inc. It incorporated 8 menu shift levels that in a restaurant would be used for changing day part pricing (happy hour, early bird dinners, etc.). We utilized those levels for the Monday through Sunday cafeteria menus plus the remaining level for a common Breakfast menu across all days. It had, as well, a polling capability through a telephone modem that we tailored so we could collect and report results at end of meals and end of day. And we were able to translate our programmed application's English checkbox instructions into the 'hexadecimal' commands the registers required.

Once we had our new "Cash Management" structure operational, we began deploying it in the company's cafeteria sites, particularly in the Healthcare sector. Of course, the financial outcomes mirrored that of our profitable pilot and soon other hospitals not under contract with our company began to inquire. As an income generator to help underwrite our evolving Information Technology Department, we began to license our application to independent customers beyond the reach of our corporate foodservice contracts. We named our system, "Common CENTS", with the 'C' in CENTS representing our Cash Management application. Later the other letters came to represent the other management aspects of our System – Expense, Nutrition, Time and Statistics.

Not long after our initial installation a hospital client came to us with a request: could we devise a way to automate a manual process that allowed their employees to charge cafeteria meal purchases and have the reimbursement taken from their payroll check as a deduction. After a widespread arduous search (before Internet and Google) we discovered an independent entrepreneur with an application that accumulated charges from MICROS registers in a Country Club setting. We arranged for his application to be adapted to our purpose and hence the "Cashless" extension of our program was born. Eventually we acquired this entrepreneur's company and embraced him as our Chief Technology Officer.

Before long the corporation's advertising firm recognized the uniqueness of our POS automation and included it in our corporate image and marketing campaigns. Ours was not the old fashioned, Food Service Company; ours was an innovative, forward thinking company that had state-of-the-art tools to significantly improve a client's operating performance. We hence changed our corporate name from Valley Food Service to Valley Innovative Food Service. And for me and my idea, the startup was well under way!

Time To Approach The Shark Tank

In a few short years through word of mouth, we had acquired more than 30 outside clients, and the licensing revenue to go along with it. These clients even included a competitor of our own corporation. Essentially, we had reached a critical mass where spinning off into a separate company made good sense. So now seemed like the logical time to approach the owners and executives to explore the possibility. I couldn't however make that approach without a well thought out map of how to get there. And along with that roadmap I had to provide ample justification for the move. The following is a brief synopsis of the steps I ensued in presenting my case and I suggest are those of anyone with similar aspirations.

a)   Document the current status of the new business concept.
The 30 plus clients already under contract, acquired without a dedicated sales or marketing effort, certainly provided ample proof of concept.

b)   Project the basic financial business model for the new venture.
Our business model incorporated residual revenues from support and maintenance fees that would not only cover our infrastructure costs, including personnel, but in time would generate reliable profits. These growing proceeds meant all net income from new software license charges or hardware and supply sales would significantly contribute to our bottom line.

c)   Delineate the economics for making the move.
At that point in time, we had built our Common CENTS team to 6

employees. By forming an independent, self-sustaining company we carved out approximately $400,000 in annual liability from the corporation's balance sheet. We appreciably reduced the corporation's labor cost, as well as travel, space and equipment overhead expenses.

d)   Ask for equity participation in the new venture.
In sales they call it asking for the order. Here it made sense to suggest that I be granted the opportunity to own some of the stock in the new company. And so, I did. After all, I reasoned, there is much greater attachment when you have skin in the game and ownership of its destiny.

Certainly, the arguments for the spinoff company were persuasive and the corporation's principles agreed. We formed a committee to decide on the corporate structure, find office space, establish accounting rules and plan the transition activities. The message is perhaps be careful what you wish for because it just may come true, and while trepidation was my initial internal reaction to their consent, I did believe I was well prepared and confident I could make a success of this new venture.

Oh, and by the way, I was extended an offer to purchase up to 20% (the maximum available for the corporation to retain the venture within the corporate ownership umbrella) of the new company's stock. I quickly seized the moment, borrowed the funds and became minority owner of Common CENTS Solutions, Inc.

Beginning The Business

Our new venture committee quickly went to work. We found reasonably priced office space to lease, relocated or acquired furniture and equipment, set up our new chart of accounts and redeployed as a separate "C Corp" business entity, which we aptly named Common CENTS Solutions, Inc. Simultaneously we began to lay the groundwork for our business plan.

In meetings with the majority owner our strategy was formulated. I referenced other IT business strategies with which I was familiar through my readings in business books and periodicals (Business Week was a favorite). I cited examples like Netscape or Amazon that sacrificed profits in early years to build their infrastructure, brand and customer base. Hence, we agreed to:

· Forego profits for the initial 5 years and instead reinvest in building the company's development and support capabilities.

· Allow losses in the initial couple of years, even in the low six figures if necessary, since they would be offset by the annual savings provided to the main corporation through separation.

· Invest in adding computer servers, application software and especially personnel to facilitate faster product development, more responsive customer support and better management.

· Position the company by the end of its fifth year to sustain reasonable profitability and growth going forward.

As it turns out it actually took us nearly seven years to posture the company for sustainable profits. And while we mostly kept our initial losses under the six-figure threshold, we did have one particularly disappointing year where we lost close to two-hundred-fifty-thousand dollars. But we survived those early years and by the end of the next seven years, Common CENTS Solutions was generating close to a million dollars a year in EBITA (Earnings Before Interest, Taxes and Amortization), a standard accounting benchmark used in the Information Technology industry.

Herding Frogs

The former Republican Leader of the United States Senate, Trent Lott, from our home state of Mississippi, once authored a book entitled "Herding Cats" in which he described the difficulties in corralling his colleagues for Senate votes. Senator Lott had to deal mostly with lawyers and while I'm certain that is an arduous task, I found aligning the technical employees of our IT business perhaps even more of a challenge; hence, the rationalization for this chapter and its title. How do you get independent thinking individuals to all work toward the common goals and objectives of the company?

In simple terms it entails the hiring process and the environment you establish to cultivate performance. There were certain practices that we followed to assure we found the most capable employees, placed them in the most suitable jobs, and provided them the motivation and guidance to enable us to best utilize their talents. To begin, our hiring philosophy can be summarized in the following terms:

· Hire the best; don't settle for less.

· Test them for aptitude; interview them for attitude.

· Focus on the trust issues; look for integrity and reliability.

· Match applicant profiles against top performer attributes.

How often have we witnessed a company with a job opening hire a mediocre candidate just so they can fill the position? I've seen it numerous times and no matter the negative repercussion, the mistake is replicated over and over again. This characteristically is a result of a well-intentioned Human Resources Department whose charge it is to fill vacant positions, but afraid of being adversely judged if those vacancies remain open for any time. Too often it is also the expedience of a department head or supervisor to complete a hiring task and rid themselves of a recruiting frustration. Is this constructive? Absolutely not! It is far better to postpone a hiring than settle for a recruit for which there may be reservations. Why? Because, an inadequate hire will have a detrimental effect on the productivity and morale of other staff as they compensate for the new employee's weaknesses. And it usually ends with the new hire either quitting because of job unhappiness or dismissed because of poor performance.

Our typical hiring process began with the standard practice of perusing resumes, screening them to identify the most plausible candidates, and inviting those who made the cut to our headquarters. But this is where we departed from standard practice. Invited candidates were informed their visit would include an initial interview and a special test we required of all recruits. Our test was not one to measure intelligence or personality traits. Nor was it a Google like puzzle test. Our unique test was specifically designed to determine an individual's thought process methodology – the logical thinking germane to problem solving. While we didn't have a pass/fail threshold, those who did well on the test invariably did well in our company. Conversely, when a supervisor took a risk on an individual with marginal results, those employees normally flamed out sooner rather than later.

Those candidates that scored well on our test were invited back for a more exhaustive interview, not only with the manager to whom the candidate would report, but other key managers as well. In this second round we evaluated the candidate's persona, probing to learn their penchant for cheerfulness, teamwork and initiative, and especially appraised for their "trust traits" like integrity and reliability. To explain our spotlight on an applicant's attitude I paraphrase the words of wisdom from Hall of Fame Coach Lou Holtz:

· Ability is what you can do.

· Motivation is what you will do.

· Attitude is how well you will do it!

The final step in our hiring process is to convene a debriefing among our managers who participated in the interviews. We discuss our assessment of the candidate, hopefully reaching a consensus to hire. In instances where an applicant was seeking a position that closely matched other similar job descriptions, we compared our perceptions of the candidate's qualities with those of our best performers, past and present. This additionally helped us gauge a candidate's chance for a successful career with the company.

Our process has certainly produced some surprisingly positive hiring outcomes along with great economic value. While we have employed many of the typical personnel as might other companies in our sphere, we have also found many employee gems that would likely not even be considered by the others. We have hired an odd sort of musicians, dispatchers, insurance adjusters and the like, all with limited experience and resumes, for open technical positions in our company. But they each showed an aptitude for our business and demonstrated an enthusiastic attitude to learn and apply acquired skills for the company's betterment.

For the Common CENTS Solutions company, we significantly reduced our new hire personnel cost. Since we were hiring inexperienced technical staff, we could start them at lower salaries. Yes, there was training to be considered with these employees, but our niche applications required training even for technically seasoned new hires, and because we provided these novice employees an opportunity not afforded them elsewhere, their enthusiasm and loyalty were unrivaled within our employee base. Of course, while we gained economies with lower starting rates for these employees, we were conscientious to compensate them competitively once their technical skills were attained and proven.

To site examples, I can point to two former musicians who were in their second decade with our company when I retired. When we interviewed the first, we found someone with a thirst for opportunity and his test result revealed a definite potential for our business. On his suggestion, we invited an associate to apply and discovered similar promise. While perhaps these two musicians dreamed of hitting the music big time, their realities led to limited jobs in retail musical instruments. Having received a chance at a second career with a prodigious upside, these individuals proved to be fast learners and in a short time both were assisting our customers with competence and compassion.

But finding and hiring the best is just the beginning. In the book "Good To Great", author Jim Collins uses the metaphor of getting the right people on your company bus. But he goes further to say it's just as important to get them in the right seats on your bus. Going back to our two musicians, the first had played keyboards and sang lead vocals, while the second remained in the supporting background of the horn section. Is it any wonder, that as their competencies grew and they evolved from our customer support department, the former ended up as a leading sales representative while the latter matured into a topnotch systems developer.

Assessing each of your employees' skills, talents and aspirations is something that must be done routinely, because as those musicians demonstrate, priorities change over time. We faithfully conducted annual performance reviews with all employees to not only formally document their personal strengths, weaknesses and attainment of goals, but to learn their level of job satisfaction and their vision for their future with the company. Beyond this annual ritual, we insisted on an open communication between supervisors and staff to facilitate more immediate feedback, particularly the praise and positive reinforcement for extraordinary effort and outcomes. In the tagline words of a hotel chain we looked to: "catch us doing right". However, just as important was the necessity to promptly instruct employees when their activities were inappropriate, or as I termed it "caring reinforcement". It was never a scolding per se, but more a counseling for their personal growth. However, there are certainly times when it's imperative to remove the resisters or incompetents less they corrupt the morale of the remaining staff.

Now that we had hired qualified employees and found their most productive positions within the company, we needed to create a thriving environment where these employees could showcase their talents yet prioritize their efforts toward the goals and aspirations of the company. Our environment was structured where employees understood their purpose, had the freedom to perform, but knew the parameters within which they must abide, and continuously strive for improvement. The following are the condensed key aspects for creating this thriving environment:

- Establish your mission
- Describe your expectations
- Set your ground rules
- Build a learning organization

Mission - The most critical facet is, I believe, establishing and communicating your company's mission. If done well the mission statement clearly conveys the most important aim for why you're in business. This statement is frequently a practical message that employees (and often the public) can easily remember and comprehend. Everyone could recite Avis's mission – "We Try Harder". And who wasn't aware of the company behind the mission – "Absolutely, Positively Overnight"?

The beauty of these statements is they are short, easy to submit to memory and convey clearly what is most important to these businesses. All too often companies devise mission statements that are full paragraphs or longer and typically have nebulous terms like: *'to be the best'* or *'leaders in our industry'*. As a consequence, by and large, it is likely no one except maybe a corporate executive can narrate it.

Our initial mission statement was perhaps a corny one. For our very first staff meeting after we separated into our own independent Common CENTS Solutions Company, I gathered our then team of six together and explained we were going to produce a pretend movie and it was going to be the antithesis of the popular movie for that (1997) time – *Get Shorty*. Our meeting even included an animated slideshow and popcorn from a local theater. The name of our movie? – *Save Shorty*.

Our damsel in distress was a Cafeteria Manager and I depicted her as a cartoon character looking frazzled and shown juggling a computer, clipboard, telephone and cash register. The plot line was that "Shorty", so named because she was short of time, personnel and resources, was drowning in details and we would be the champions to rescue her with our imaginative applications, installation assistance, and caring support. Hence "Save Shorty" became our mission statement.

Was that corny? Yes, guilty as charged! But was there motive behind my madness? Absolutely! Considering we were forming a new entrepreneurial company with employees formerly working in a large stodgy corporate environment, I first wanted to send a message that this atmosphere would be quite different. While we had serious business to conduct, I wanted it to be fun at the same time. Of course, this is not inconsistent with the way many other technology companies operate. It is well documented that a less rigid, more relaxed working environment releases the creative powers of the technical employee. And if there's one phenomenon that gets a knowledge worker's focus, especially those with the service attitude like we hired, it's an opportunity to be altruistic.

I intentionally aimed for a brief mission statement so that any employee could easily submit it to memory. But what about that silly Shorty cartoon? This too had a purpose. Beside the fun aspect, I wanted to imprint an image so top-of-mind that when a customer called, that image immediately popped into the psyche of our responder and triggered thought of our mission statement, "Save Shorty". And for anyone snickering at this moment, consider Google's homepage along with its many whimsical historical variations. I'm sure the silly Google homepage image is vivid in each of our minds eye. From my viewpoint, this concept worked as well as I had hoped and we built a whole theme around it. For instance, in our monthly staff meetings we included a session called 'Shorty Says' where we would discuss feedback, good and bad, from our customers.

But as our company matured and we developed a more diverse array of applications, including a hotel style room service system for hospital patients, we needed a more refined and public mission statement. But certainly, I wanted to retain the altruistic concept behind our Save Shorty theme. This refinement resulted in our new mission statement: "Making Life Better for our Customers and Theirs". In other words, while we continued to provide solutions beneficial to an organizations management, ala "Save Shorty", our systems had practical benefit for the eventual users, whether that was satisfying employees by expediting the cafeteria line or pleasing hospital patients with room service.

Our new mission permeated our entire organization from our design of intuitive applications to the amenable responsiveness by our Sales and Support teams. While "Save Shorty" served its purpose at the beginning as an internal mission statement, our new revised mission statement was one that we could advertise outside the company to explain to our markets the rationale for our existence.

Expectations – Another important function in setting up a high performance environment is clearly identifying what you expect from your employees. I summarized my expectations in something called our Seepee Teepee, characterized by the image of a leaky Indian teepee. Although we evolved a more serious mission statement, that didn't mean we had to do away with whimsy like the Seepee Teepee. But it was actually a synonym for a set of initials – CPTP – which equated to the first letters of our four fundamental principles, Customers, Profits, Teamwork, and Personal Growth. These tenets were our company's support posts, just as four tent poles are needed to erect a teepee.

Once our employees assimilated these tenets there was little requisite for micromanagement. Employees understood that superior customer service was paramount if we wanted to distinguish our company and grow sales and revenues. They were cognizant as well that they had to watch their spending and bill all services rendered if we were to meet our profit goals. They were aware of their obligation to be team players if we wanted to maximize productivity. And they understood that continuous learning was for the betterment of their careers and the company's long-term performance.

Ground Rules – Of course I did set some definite parameters to which I was resolute that our employees would respect. The two most prevalent were:

· Customer satisfaction is everyone's job. I was insistent that all employees respond to customer communications promptly. That meant to begin, answering the phone personally whenever possible. But in those cases where messages were left on voice mail, I counted on our staff to reply quickly. So too for customer emails. There is nothing as frustrating for a customer as leaving a message without getting a confirming response. The customer is left to wonder whether anyone actually received it or even cared. Even for a difficult customer problem that can't be solved quickly, it makes better sense to proactively inform the customer of its progress rather than wait for the infuriated customer's follow up call that is sure to come when no communications are forthcoming.

· Fix it the first time; don't let it linger. Haven't we all brought our vehicles to the repair shop only to return multiple times before a problem is actually fixed? This is certainly irritating to the customer, but more so it is truly unproductive as time is wasted attending to a repeat issue instead of moving to a more fruitful event. To accomplish this objective employees have to think rather than simply react. For customer service issues, employees must consider the underlying cause that triggered the issue. It's not enough to just apply a quick fix or work around. It's crucial to discover and cure the causal factors so the customer's operation is not corrupted again in the future.

Learning Organization – The true secret to an enduring, high performing business is acquiring the disciplines of 'The Learning Organization'. This is the concept of management thinking espoused in a book titled "The Fifth Discipline" by author Peter M. Senge. While Mr. Senge's teachings are too extensive to do them justice within this book, the most salient points to consider are these core disciplines:

1.   Systems Thinking – the ability to see a business system in its entirety rather than as isolated components.

2.   Personal Mastery – a special level of proficiency whereby, individuals consistently learn and improve their understanding.

3.   Mental Models – a challenge to deeply ingrained assumptions and generalizations that impede a greater insight.

4.   Shared Vision – a common picture of the organization's future that all members share.

5.   Team Learning – the capacity to produce a team intelligence more powerful than its collective members.

The Learning Organization wisdom delineated in "The Fifth Discipline" is quite substantial, and having worked in that environment I can testify how exhilarating and potent this method of operation can be to the success of a business.

Creating A Brand

Now that we had our company set up, long range plans made and staff hired, it was time to turn attention to branding. What perception did we want potential customers to have of our company and products? How would we differentiate our company and products from our competitors?

The first consideration for creating our "brand" was a no-brainer. Our company name, Common CENTS Solutions was a reflection of our intent to offer systems that were sensible and economical. And these attributes were intrinsic to our R&D. As prime example, consider the advancement of our new generation of applications that took place at the start of Y2K:

Our initial applications were designed around Microsoft's Disk Operating System (DOS). The nature of DOS made it the ideal platform for applications suited to non-technical users because it required step by step user interaction. Since our applications were utilized by foodservice workers more familiar with cambros than computers, this DOS sequential selection process made it easy for these neophytes to understand and choose program actions.

However, in the late 90's, Microsoft had introduced newer Windows Operating Systems and our competitors were all reorienting their programs for that environment. We therefore were also pressed to convert our applications to Windows. But after strategy sessions with our Chief Technology Officer, it was our consensus that Windows wouldn't contribute significantly to our applications' performance, but instead would make it more difficult for our users to operate .... when to right click, double click, etc. After thoughtful consideration and in keeping with our "common sense" development track, we chose a different direction.

Our research indicated that an evolving technology for Internet apps might suit our goal. Browser-based design at that time was bleeding edge and there was considerable risk for whether this technology would actually be adopted. We contracted with an advisory consultant and after several R&D brainstorming sessions, our Chief Technology Officer went about designing our next generation applications. As it turns out of course, browser-based programs became universally accepted and soon everyone was using the Internet for business, entertainment, shopping, etc. Quickly our new generation of browser-based applications became as easy to use as our former DOS apps because it was as familiar as the Internet.

Our second branding factor was inherently connected to our mission "Making Life Better for our Customers and Theirs". Execution of this mission obligated us to extend our brand beyond our applications. It meant our software had to be unfailing, our hardware reliable, our support responsive and our maintenance dependable. To fashion this element of our brand identification we had to live up to these benchmarks each and every day. These brand operating standards permeated our entire organization from the careful design of our products to our caring assistance during installations.

Finally, though, we needed a way to differentiate our products from our competitors. We needed to clearly demonstrate why our company's solutions were a better choice than the others. And we needed an effective way to communicate that difference to our Healthcare marketplace. Our answers would be derived from the amalgamation of market research we had conducted both past and present.

Starting with the past, one of our first actions before we launched our separate enterprise was to commission our marketing firm to survey the Healthcare Foodservice landscape. Our goal was to:

· Determine awareness of our company and products.
· Confirm prospective customer needs and aspirations.
· Ascertain the entrenchment of competitive systems.

We discovered that Common CENTS Solutions had very little recognition in the Healthcare market. And while we integrated within our solution the MICROS point-of-sale platform, the worldwide leading brand in the Hospitality industry, this register system didn't even make the top 10 in what hospitals implemented in their cafeterias. We also learned that Healthcare foodservice operators did endorse the real value of a solution like ours and that there was not a dominate provider.

We combined this information with our own research on the trends emerging in the Healthcare foodservice sector. In our study we found that hospitals were replacing the old sterile cafeteria design with greater restaurant style services. Stainless steel serving lines were being replaced by colorful scramble type décor; standard meat and three only choices had been upgraded with pizza, deli and display cooking stations among others. In general, Hospital foodservice operations were transitioning to a more retail orientation and we saw this as our opportunity to distinguish our brand. After all, from our inception we had been integrating best restaurant practices within our solutions. In our cafeteria cash management application, we included retail concepts like menu engineering and innovations like digital menu boards. In our patient room service application, we pioneered advancements like touchscreen order taking and kitchen production displays. All of this coalesced into the marketing theme we adopted: *"Bringing Hospitality to Healthcare"*.

This slogan became our mantra in all our advertising. Through our consistent execution of these three facets of our branding efforts, we soon gained a reputation as an innovative, caring, state-of-the-art company. This was certainly in sharp contrast to our stolid, legacy prone competition.

Pricing Strategies

As mentioned previously our company name, *Common CENTS Solutions,* was conceived with the intent to provide sensible solutions at economical prices. But what exactly is an economical price? That is perhaps the hardest of all questions to answer, especially as a startup. We put considerable thought into our pricing strategies, some of which were spot on from the start and others that had to evolve over time. We had two major strategy sectors:

- General Pricing Policies
- Product and Service Pricing Practices

Our solutions commonly consisted of several elements. They included application software, computer and system hardware, delivery, training, implementation, software support, hardware maintenance and programming services. Later in this chapter I will focus on the pricing practices we developed for these individual products and services. But to start, it is meaningful to know that we most often proposed our solution as an assemblage of these independent elements into a total package requiring capital funding by our customers. Occasionally we were authorized to separate facets of our package that qualified under a customer's annual operating budget, thereby reducing the capital investment. So, with that in mind, the following overview describes our General Pricing Policies.

From the beginning we established certain standards for how we set our pricing:

- · Return On Investment (ROI) Formulation
- · Scaled Price Configurations
- · Steadfast Price Lists
- · Guaranteed Satisfaction

We had done enough market research to learn that hospital administrators would straightforwardly approve capital purchases if they had a return on investment of two years or less. That then became the basis for general pricing of our solutions. Our original product was a cafeteria cash management application running in conjunction with a Micros point-of-sale platform. And as our initial customer implementations demonstrated our application increased their revenue a minimum 10% as a result. However, since this revenue increase was actually lost revenue recaptured, due to theft, mistakes and register shortcomings, all of it went directly to the bottom line as ROI profit. For our add-on cashless payment application, we discovered at least 20% in sales increases, which after factoring out the food cost translated into half as the ROI. Hence, we could reasonably estimate a two-year ROI for each solution and likewise formulate our application license fees based on the volumes of our typical hospital client. This calculation set our baseline for our application license fees.

But we performed a couple of other benchmarks before formally setting our pricing structure. Once we had each license fee baseline, based on the two-year ROI formula, we measured it against our competitors' prices for similar configurations. Because we were new to the market, we intended to price our products slightly (10% to 20%) below our competition. Fortunately, for the most part, our ROI formulation accomplished that goal without change, but when necessary we did consider some fine-tuning. Lastly before we formally fixed our pricing, we appraised it for our company's profit margins. Our profit margin (total expected sale revenue less total estimated costs) had to be significant enough to sustain our company without compromising our high level of customer support. Provided a product's pricing supported company margins that met or surpassed our coveted threshold, it was locked in. If the pricing fell below our desired margins, we would adjust it through a compromise in one or all of the three formulation factors – rate of customer investment return, competitive advantage and/or our generated profit margin.

A second strategy we initiated was to have scaled application price configurations. Scaled pricing meant we could start with a minimum base configuration and commensurate application license fee then add components a-la-carte, so that small hospitals wouldn't have to pay inflated fees for capabilities they might never use while larger hospitals could scale up to take advantage of the application's full scope to suit their needs. This strategy also allowed us to be a bit more competitive than our rivals who often bundled their products and pricing.

A third preliminary decision starting out was to set firm pricing and only offer discounts based upon volume purchases, and even those were fixed at certain percentages for certain volume levels. This empowered the sales team to honestly proclaim to prospective customers that they were receiving the exact same pricing as any other customer, barring those buying multiple systems. It also helped us prove our brand as a company of integrity and eliminated the individual "back room" deals for which I personally deplored. It did take a strong backbone to stand firm on a proposal price in the face of client pressure, but more than a few times customers expressed their appreciation for our truth in pricing.

But alas, this firm price list strategy was eventually abandoned by edict from an ensuing majority shareholder who couldn't appreciate the wisdom in it and held a false impression instead that back-office discounting would accelerate sales. Over time sales actually deteriorated, primarily because this discounting served to devalue the offering and prospective customers began to sense that it must be a flawed product. And of course, these confidentially negotiated discounted deals had a significant adverse effect on our profits. We finally came back around to a standardized pricing model through the use of a programmed checklist template, but we did include some greater liberty, allowing the sales team to offer restrained discounts based upon their assessment of competitive pressures. Sure enough, sales returned and just prior to my departure, sales were growing by 20% year on year, even though we were in the depths of the "Great Recession" that started in 2008.

One exclusive we built into our pricing policies was our satisfaction guarantee. Our guarantee stated that if for any reason a customer was not satisfied with our solution within the first six months of utilization, they could return our system and we would refund all of their hardware and software investment and relieve them from the contract. Any of our programming, installation and/or training out-of-pocket expenses were not refundable. There were two reasons for instituting this policy: 1) to build instant credibility in our solution since customers were not locked in, and 2) because we had total confidence in the soundness of our solutions and our ability to support our products. While none of our competitors were brave enough to match our guarantee, for us it turned out to be a no-brainer, since in our 15-year existence, Common CENTS Solutions had not a single customer act on it or even threaten to do so. But this outcome was not so remarkable if you really think about it. Once a customer had committed to our solution and expended the sweat equity to install it, wouldn't it have to be a truly awful experience before the customer would forfeit that effort? While we may have had an occasional misstep in our support, our overall customer's experience was always positive. Surprisingly I noticed that an apparel manufacturer offered a year's satisfaction guarantee on a pair of cargo shorts I recently purchased at a big box store. As I contemplated this guarantee it occurred to me how smart this strategy was. While the brand was well known (Wrangler), its value pricing gave pause about its quality. The guarantee offered reassurance to overcome that hesitation. Yet in the end after all, who among us would even remember this guarantee a month after the purchase?

As a final note, I must mention an innovative financing plan we came up with around the midlife of our existence to help hospitals navigate around their capital budgeting difficulties. We named it the Midas Plan and it encouraged sales we might not have otherwise secured. In essence it was a true rental plan without the long-term commitment of a purchase or lease. Hospitals therefore could pay for our system out of their operating funds and avoid the arduous capital budget approval process altogether. While this rental was and likely remains unique to our industry, it made good sense because the payback from our inflated rental priced solutions were more than ample to recoup our investment and produce healthy profits in a reasonably short timeframe. Yet, it still allowed a respectable financial return for the hospital. The major risk in this type of financing was a customer's possible bankruptcy before we received our full cost recovery, but how many larger hospitals have ever gone out of business? The answer was less than one-tenth of one percent. I'd say that is a pretty safe bet!

That summarizes our general pricing policies, but what about the pricing practices for each type of product and service we offered:

1. Application Software
2. Hardware Systems
3. Software Support
4. Hardware Maintenance
5. Programming, Implementation and Training Services
6. Setup and Delivery Services

Product and service pricing entails an abundance of detail that could prove confusing. Therefore, here I will provide an abridged version of our pricing methodologies with their justifications.

But first a little background: Our mainstay product for which we based the success of the company was our application software. The other products and services were mostly ancillary to the sale of our software. The exception was our Point-of-Sale hardware systems. At the beginning of our venture we were acquiring our Micros POS equipment through a local dealer, but that dealer also represented several other brands to the chagrin of the Micros' corporate management. Shortly after forming our independent Common CENTS Solutions enterprise, Micros Systems, Inc. approached us with an offer to become their exclusive Mississippi authorized dealer. What induced them to advocate for this arrangement was our decision to integrate our applications solely on the Micros POS line of products. As it happened, we became more familiar with the programming and repair of their Micros devices than even their then current local dealer. Consequentially our decision to standardize on a single POS product line proved to have benefits unforeseen at the time.

Since acceptance of the Micros offer would provide us favorable dealer product costing and access to their corporate technical and support networks, we readily agreed. However, acceptance also meant assuming responsibility for selling and supporting Micros POS systems in the local Hospitality market. While our niche was in Healthcare Foodservice, we also became more expert in the restaurant and hotel businesses. But as hospitals evolved into a more hospitality orientation, this experience certainly benefited our competitive posture. Now for our pricing practices:

Application Software: We've already explained how we formulated the pricing for our application software. What is important to recognize is that we did not sell our software, but rather we leased the use of it. The one-time price we charged was for the license to use the software. This is the same principle applied when you download an eBook to your Kindle or a music iTune to your iPod. Unlike the past where you could buy a music record or CD, the 99 cents you pay for a song from the Apple store only allows you to "borrow" it, not buy and own it. Additionally, aside from our application initial license fee, we had an annual subscription fee (ASF) that if accepted provided ongoing updates to the software and technical support to resolve system issues and fix software bugs. I will discuss the details of the ASF in an upcoming paragraph.

Our licensing arrangement began with a fee for the core application, then affixed supplementary license fees for hardware device connections and/or additional software modules. If a Healthcare client for our room service application wanted to include mobile devices for taking patient orders at the bedside and add our tray tracking software module to verify meal deliveries, they would pay an initial licensing fee for the core room service software and accompanying license fees for each mobile device and the add-on tray tracking module. In several cases we created "kits" with favorable pricing that packaged together common configurations with appeal to a broad array of prospective customers. This strategy was welcomed by customers because they could acquire a "right-sized" configuration and not pay for more than they required. For us it bolstered our competitive pricing and kept us in touch with customers as they grew and upgraded, providing ample opportunity to sell new and additional applications.

Hardware Systems: Since we were a Micros Systems Dealer, we received advantageous product cost that we put to our competitive benefit. Our main competitor happened to incorporate the same Micros POS equipment in their offerings, but because they were a VAR (value added reseller) they acquired their equipment through the dealer network at higher costs then marked it up further for their own resale. We adopted the Micros' manufactures suggested retail pricing (MSRP) and still made reasonable margins from our hardware sales. Better yet again, it placed us in a marketing posture where our solution pricing could undercut this competitor since they had artificially higher prices to capture the margins they desired.

We utilized this hardware pricing strategy in a few other ways to improve our marketing capabilities. First, when we found ourselves involved in a large customer sale, we could discount our hardware pricing to leverage it as a "loss leader" (although we still captured nominal margins) to better the odds of acquiring the business and the lucrative software fees associated with it. Secondly, with acquisition of these large business opportunities our Micros published MSRP pricing lent credibility to our image and customer confidence in our ethical business practices. For instance, we enjoyed a long-term relationship with Hospital Corporation of America (HCA) as their sole provider for applicable software and among the reasons was their comfort that our pricing was rational, fair and trustworthy.

<u>Software Support:</u> As referenced earlier, with the license of our application software we also offered an Annual Subscription Fee (ASF) for our support of the software system. Initially we calculated our ASF as 20% of the initial license fee, even though 15% was customary throughout our application software industry. We chose this higher percentage because our entry license fee was purposely lower to gain market share. Once we were an established player in our niche business and could demand a greater license fee, we reduced our ASF to the 15% normal. Both the early and later ASF percentages were formulated to produce enough revenue to fund the appropriate staffing for superior service as well as produce a reasonable profit, but we also built in a little extra for a customer appreciation surprise. From day one we set out on a course to distinguish ourselves from our competitors and decided to send an unexpected token gift each holiday season to each customer as a thank you for their business. In Louisiana they call this lagniappe. For our ASF customers we distributed tins of premium mixed nuts, purchased from a local civic club, to be shared among our customer's staff. Not only did customers find this expression of gratitude exceptional, our monies went to supporting good works within our local community.

This annual subscription provided remote technical support to answer customer questions, convey operational advice and fix software failures. The subscription also entitled customers to software release updates without additional charge. The fee was predicated upon contracted hours of service according to multiple plans starting with our standard 8 to 5, Monday through Friday and stair-stepping up to our complete 24/7 coverage. We made it mandatory during the first year to at least include our standard subscription coverage, but optional thereafter. For support service requested beyond the contracted hours we had a premium per minute charge billed in 15 minute minimum blocks. However, for customers already under an ASF contract these charges were discounted by 50%. For customers not on an ASF contract these quarter hour charges could quickly overtake the cost of the subscription. And if a customer discontinued the subscription service not only would coverage revert to the per-minute charge, but the service would be terminated altogether once the software lapsed into two update releases behind. This practice was instituted to strengthen our support capability by not wasting time troubleshooting issues that had been already resolved in subsequent software releases.

At the termination point, the customer's only option to reestablish software coverage would be to license a new current copy of the application software at the expense of another initial license fee. With these incentives and consequences, it was rare for a customer to reject our subscription service. Hence, our ASF became a laudable and stable source of residual revenue. As importantly for our customers, it kept their systems operating unimpeded and their applications updated with the newest features, which in turn kept their endorsements of our company flowing.

Hardware Maintenance: Unlike our software support that could be conducted remotely on-line, hardware maintenance required the physical touching of a malfunctioning device, mostly through an on-site visit. This presented a unique challenge since we had customers spread throughout the US. We conquered this challenge via two channels. Since we utilized the Micros line of POS equipment exclusively within our solution and as an authorized Micros Dealer ourselves, we could delegate the maintenance to the dealer closest to our customer. Our other option was a depot maintenance arrangement whereby the customer would ship the defective component to our repair department and we would return it after repairs were made.

Our practice was to provide a hardware equipment warranty during the first year of operation, so that our maintenance contract was required only upon the anniversary of the installation date and each year thereafter. While this warranty was primarily based on a pass-through of the hardware manufacturers' warranty, different peripheral device (printers, scales, etc.) manufacturers extended dissimilar terms - some offered as little as a 90-day warranty while others provided a 3-year warranty. We found that customers liked the simplification and stability of a year's guaranteed hardware performance, so we chose to take the risk on shorter warranties and the advantages of the longer ones to standardize it all into a single one-year warranty.

Like the support service for our software, we offered multiple annual maintenance plans depending upon the desired hours of service from our standard 8 to 5 to our complete 24/7. Each incremental coverage plan came with an escalating percentage up-charge except for the depot plan which entailed a discount. But it was further complicated by the proximity of the customer's location in relation to the nearest Micros service office. In this instance we had additional percentage up-charges for measured mileage "zones" beyond our standard plan's 30 mile radius. And finally, we had to make allowances for out-of-scope (not covered within the contract) billings. These were time and material charged services which included hourly charges for normal business hours as well as escalating rates for afterhours and on weekends and holidays.

Income attributed to our hardware maintenance agreements was derived certainly from our local on-site maintenance contracts and our depot maintenance contracts, but even when we assigned a contract to another dealer, we retained 20% of the revenue to remain the first point of contact for those customers. Because of the reliability of the Micros platform this income source became a significant contributor to our profitability.

Programming, Installation, and Training: Nicknamed PIT, these charges primarily covered the services related to the implementation of our application software and any related equipment, but PIT also addressed similar services requested beyond implementation. True to our Common CENTS Solutions name, we originated a new method for charging customers for PIT services.

The norm for our industry was to itemize each PIT function separately and tack on travel expense invoices as an afterthought. Customers had difficulty with this charging technique, first because they weren't able to pinpoint an absolute cost for budgeting purposes and second because implementations were dynamic and unsuited to fixed timelines for each PIT function. Conversely, we devised a blueprint allowing us to quote a single turnkey PIT charge, including all travel expenses, and guaranteed a successful implementation.

To begin we built metrics for the time required to complete known pre-installation tasks such as building the back-office computer server or initializing and loading the database. We translated these metrics into the number of man/days, both internal and at the customer's site, to complete the implementation project. We then factored in a daily travel cost for the on-site days. In the end we had a flat PIT quote that customers could depend upon and one flexible enough for us to adjust resources accordingly. Post implementation PIT services for special programming requests or additional training when conducted remotely were charged by the hour based on the internal man/day rate divided by 10 (hours per man/day). Any post implementation PIT services requested on site were quoted at the on-site man/day rate with a two-day minimum charge.

A beneficial offshoot from our bundled PIT model was elimination of the laborious accounting exercise to capture and bill back all the associated travel expenses. These travel expenses represented less than 10% of the total implementation costs, but consumed a majority of the billing effort. Reporting each travel expense and generating customer invoices with appropriate documentation attached required copious man hours to produce and resolve. Because we buffered our anticipated travel expenses into our single implementation PIT quotation, we not only eliminated this accounting nightmare, but we actually garnered a small added profit by prudently managing our travel spending.

Setup & Delivery: As part of our proposals we incorporated a setup and delivery charge to cover the staging and shipping of any computer servers and/or point-of-sale equipment. Because our systems almost always included point-of-sale terminals, our charge was calculated as a cost per each terminal with an additional surcharge built in to pay team implementation bonuses. I will discuss this implementation bonus along with other incentives and compensations for our employees in a later chapter in this series.

As you can attest through this posting, pricing practices are an expansive topic and there are many more nuances that I could have discussed, but this post captures the salient points.

Employee Compensation Systems

As was dialoged in an earlier chapter, I strived to establish an employee friendly environment that offered fun yet challenging work. I also believed it was important for our team members to have the opportunity to balance their work and private lives. Much of our compensation, incentive and benefit programs were aimed at providing employees a rewarding work experience that conveyed a genuine concern for both their personal and professional well beings. But if this ambition was to become reality it was imperative that we build a thriving, profitable business. Our company's vision statement summed up my roadmap for achieving these goals. Basically, it follows the same philosophy of deceased motivational guru, Zig Ziglar, who said: "You can have everything you want in life if you just give enough other people what they want".

Our Company's Vision was to provide:

Customers with innovative solutions of tangible value in a trouble-free operating environment;
Employees with meaningful work and business growth to allow them to reach their full potential; and
Shareholders with profits attained through ethical business practices enough to perpetuate our vision and yield reasonable returns on their investment.

By giving these "other" people what they wanted I was confident I would beget the environment for which I aspired.........and sure enough that is what happened.

Salaries – Any compensation discussion, I surmise, starts with salaries. As was mentioned prior our M.O. was finding qualified staff in search of an opportunity and hiring them at moderate starting pay rates. But to fulfill the promise of compensating employees according to acquired skills, we had to do an annual comparison of pay rates for similar positions with like skills and raise our candidates within these competitive ranges, else risk losing them. Most often we could retain our salaries on the lower or middle point of the range because employees valued our passionate and compassionate culture. Unsurprisingly this approach of lower initial salaries and competitive but judicious annual adjustments helped keep our labor costs well contained. Of course, one way we supplemented employees was with creative benefit and recognition programs and monetary incentives in return for their contributions to the company's welfare.

Benefits – Certainly we offered the company benefits expected in our competitive environment, like major medical along with other supplemental insurances, 401K retirement plans, continuing education programs, and paid time off for vacation, holiday and sick. We also provided employees with the necessary tools and equipment to perform their roles proficiently and welcomed new hires onto the team with a set of company logo apparel.

Employee medical insurance has been a major expense for all companies that grant it, and although we were a relatively small enterprise with 30 employees, we remained committed to providing this benefit for our employees. We covered each employee with a comprehensive single plan with reasonable deductibles and co-pays, and required they contribute only a nominal portion of the premium. They could easily expand to family coverage for an additional premium fee. Our 401K Plan was typical of most retirement plans and included a company match. Our Continuing Education Program not only reimbursed tuition expenses for qualified courses and grade attainment, but we liberally encouraged attendance at conferences and seminars related to job skill improvements. After all, personal growth was the last of the success tenants we espoused – remember the Seepee Teepee (CPTP)?

For holidays we offered the basic six. Instead of sick time, we allotted personal time off that could be used for sickness, but also perhaps for childcare needs, doctor appointments or personal emergencies. We allotted 5 personal days per year and permitted employees to accrue up to 40 days for time not taken. This last arrangement was intended to cover any employee that may have contacted an extended illness or had an accident that incapacitated them for an extended length. In a worst case scenario this accrual provided a bridge until long term disability insurance kicked in. With so many traveling employees, accidents were a real possibility. Vacation time off was tiered based on years of service – 2, 3, & 4 weeks of vacation for 1, 5, & 10 years of employment respectively. And when work schedules interfered with vacation schedules, we allowed employees to carry over untaken vacation time into the new year by up to half of their previous year's approved amount.

I was confident that our employees truly appreciated that we constructed our benefits for the employee and not just as a "me too" cost of business.

After all, consider that in 2013 according to the Associated Press, 40% of private sector workers, or 40 million individuals, didn't get paid time off. Companies not providing paid time off may be deceiving themselves into thinking they're saving money, but during, epidemics like flu season, their workers are likely coming to work sick rather than lose a day's pay, thereby infecting others, and costing these companies more through lost productivity than any hoped for savings. The result of our generous paid time off policy was a significant reduction in sick time as compared to industry standards. Most, if not all, business gurus advocate customer loyalty as a key to building a successful company, but gaining customer loyalty actually starts by securing employee loyalty and thoughtful benefits certainly helped us toward those ends.

Travel – How often have we all heard company spokespersons say "employees are our most important assets"? Well one good way to test the sincerity of their claim is to look at their travel policies. Do they strike an equitable balance between expense control and respect for those important assets? Here's a chance to judge our travel policies:

· For air travel we allowed each employee to retain their airline bonus miles, but we insisted that they choose the lowest fare airline or a comparable rate from another depending upon route efficiency. For us this often meant Southwest Airlines for the cities to which they directly connected, or Delta Airlines when rates were competitive and/or destinations were beyond those of Southwest. Of course, coach was our norm but many employees earned free first class upgrades through their priority club memberships. Anyone that has flown since 9-11 recognizes the frustrating nuisance air travel has become, so allowing the employee frequent flyer miles perk showed our appreciation for their efforts extended on the company's behest.

· Through our corporate Hertz Rental Car agreement, we allowed the rental of standard size automobiles. I've seen many companies restrict their "valued" employees to compact size cars while their executives drove luxuries. I believed that today's travel is such a hassle that the cost of a standard car upgrade for our most important assets was a small price to pay, and certainly it fostered employee loyalty.

· For overnight stays we authorized middle-of-the-road Hampton Inn hotel accommodations. And we permitted private rooms, rather than the doubling-up requirement of some other firms. Our employees were on the road so often that I deemed giving employees a home away from home where the surroundings were comfortable and familiar, regardless of the city, reduced job stress and increased performance. Hampton Inn ideally fit that profile for us, and while not the cheapest, rates were generally reasonable. Again, we let employees retain any free stays they earned.

· Meal allowances were quite an interesting phenomenon. When we first formed our new company, we adopted the travel meals reimbursement policy from our former parent corporation, which allowed up to $45 per day for receipted meals. The problem surfaced when we acknowledged that some employees were spending their full daily allowance, unseen on the receipts, more for beverages than for food. Keep in mind that we employed a disproportionate number of young, single males due to our intense travel demands, so dinner receipts seemed too often to come from a "Hooters" restaurant. My concern was that these employees could perhaps be jeopardizing their safety by driving somewhat impaired at night in a strange city, and certainly could be less alert for their morning job activities. So, we devised a per diem meal reimbursement plan that paid employees $42 per day while out of town and what they didn't spend was theirs to pocket. As it turned out the extra cash potential proved meaningful to our employees, especially our new-hires and served to promote healthier afterhours choices. And in practice this policy change not only substantiated our contention that it wouldn't cost the company a dime extra, it even saved us a few bucks.

· Our mostly younger, unmarried workforce also presented another unusual challenge for me. Often, while our employees were geeky smart, they didn't always do well with their personal finances. Some was attributed to the naivety of youth and undisciplined spending; some was the lack of enough time to establish good credit. This left many a worthy employee without the resources to pay their travel expenses and unable generally to qualify for a personal credit card. Therefore, we arranged through American Express a personal credit card for each employee with a company guarantee for the payments. This enabled a seamless conduct of our business, yet gave us reimbursement protection via a final payroll check settlement in the case of dismissal or resignation.

These travel policies, especially our per diem meal reimbursement schedule, are examples of a 'Learning Organization' at work, analyzing problems in a broader scope, thinking outside the box and implementing solutions that affect positive change, sometimes without cost. A typical kneejerk reaction to our meal allowance concern would have been to micromanage the meal expense submissions, adding administrative and audit overhead and likely not even accomplishing the objective.

It is also prudent to remember that because we billed customers on a fixed daily rate that incorporated our anticipated travel charges (discussed in the 'Pricing Strategy' chapter) it gave us the flexibility to implement these travel policies. And because the recruitment of competent staff was extremely competitive in our business, our travel policies gave us a little leg up in the process.

Recognition – I include employee recognition among this chapter on compensation, not because there is any financial reward involved, but rather because it is one of the most underappreciated benefits of any company and perhaps the one with the most enduring payback. There are studies galore that espouse the virtues of employee recognition for outstanding performance, and we inculcated it as standard management practice both direct to the employee verbally and broadcast to the organization through electronic media. One particular award of note was what we aptly named the 'Success Starts With You' cube. Yes, it was literally a cube. Made of clear Lucite, it had the word Success prominently etched on the front and some characteristics leading to that end inscribed within – Integrity, Goals, Opportunity, and Commitment. We awarded it at our staff meeting to any employee that demonstrated extraordinary performance. While this performance may have been conducted toiling on an internal company project, most often it was in the service to our customers. As a word of caution, in order to maintain the integrity of this type recognition, it was never awarded to curry favor with an employee or to appease a department head or for any reason less than intended. Once awarded for anything other than an extraordinary effort it loses its value and employees quickly perceive it as a guise.

Incentives – Financial incentives have always been a part of business motivation, especially in the sales arena. However, admit it or not, the financial rewards given to sales people have always been a source of contention. Often, I had caught disgruntled comments from support team members asking why Sales gets all the glory while they get all the work. Conversely, sales commissions have been such a standard across all businesses that it would be extremely difficult recruiting good sales professionals without them.

I believe that financial incentives are a good motivator, not just for sales people, but for others too within the organization. But I also deem that any financial incentive has to be anchored on an objective, quantifiable set of criteria. I should also mention my resolve that if an incentive is to have maximum impact, it must be simple enough for the intended party to track and calculate. Here was my interpretation of the financial incentives we provided:

Sales – To begin it is important to know that for our technical systems, it required a consultative sales approach. This meant hiring a sales force with a certain level of starting expertise and that meant paying for that expertise. Our sales team's compensation included an ample base salary supplemented by their commissions. Generally, a fair salesperson would earn commissions equal to half their salary, an average salesperson would earn an amount equal to their salary and an outstanding salesperson would earn double their salary. For clarity sake, the statement above equivocates to total compensation of 150%, double and triple their base salary respectively.

As delineated in the previous 'Pricing Strategies' chapter, we value priced our systems based on the customer's ROI and initially we didn't authorize any discounting. But at the insistence of our ensuing majority (financial investor) owner, discounting became customary. Accordingly, I had to adjust our commission schedule to buffer this trend or suffer significant profit loss. So, I formulated a commission plan that paid 12% on the sale of our application software and 2.5% on the equipment hardware. The commission difference between software and hardware was predicated on the reduced margins associated with the hardware. However, to discourage discounting on the application software I revised the commission formula so that for each 1% price discount, there was a corresponding 0.15% reduction in sales commission paid on the net sale price. The translation went like this: for a software sale of $50K the commission would be $6,000 (12%), but discounted 20% to a price of $40K the commission would be reduced by 3% (20 X .15%) and only pay $3,600 (9% X $40K). So, as you can extrapolate, a 20% price discount meant a 40% commission drop. As I will explain in an upcoming chapter on selling, this commission policy was not unreasonable, because at our value pricing with proper sales technique, discounting wasn't warranted. Discounting is the first option a salesperson will revert to when they haven't followed a proper or thorough sales campaign.

We did distribute end-of-year bonuses when stretch sales targets were attained and we conducted periodic sales contests to promote friendly competition among the sales team.

Support – For our Support Team members we had two financial incentives. For those assigned to the on-site implementation of our systems after the sale, we paid bonuses commensurate to the project's scope. Because all of our systems included terminals in their configurations, we authorized the bonus as an accumulated amount per terminal ($200 initially), so that the larger the project and number of terminals, the greater the bonus. However, this bonus was only paid when the implementation was judged successful according to a customer quality survey taken upon project completion. The customer's score had to rate very good to excellent before the bonus was authorized. The bonus was also apportioned among the on-site implementation team members, so that everyone had a stake in its success. The payment apportionment and quality survey benchmark provided the project leader the inducement to perform the installation as lean as was practical without jeopardizing its quality.

For the Support Team members remaining in-house to handle customer service requests, we provided a 5% commission on any justifiable billing. This program evolved when we discovered that all our services were not being adequately charged back to the customers. Apparently, our staff was so ingrained with customer satisfaction that they often felt obliged to provide their services gratis, particularly afterhours. And not only did they get kudos from our customers for their hospitable and "generous" service, they eliminated the paperwork labor to initiate the billing. While I personally was not a fan of paying an incentive to get staff to perform what I saw as their responsibility, once we implemented this program our helpdesk revenue increased about 20%.

One point of note – although we had a couple of dedicated helpdesk support personnel, most of our support staff was segmented into platoons. This allowed us to alternate implementation teams each week. Ideally individuals would be on an install one week and in the office the next. The thought was that during the off weeks in-house those individuals who just completed installations would then be available to answer support calls, most of which would customarily come from those newest customers. Secondly, the off week afforded them time to prepare for the next upcoming installation. This schema reinforced our pledge to balance the employee's work and home life.

R & D and Administration – For these staff members we found it problematic defining measurable criteria on which to formulate a bonus plan. We dabbled with benchmarks like programming lines of code or inventory turns or receivable collections, but none could account for the proficiency or efficiency in which the task was accomplished. So in lieu of a defined plan, we authorized spot bonuses from time to time based on company performance and a subjective appraisal by management. Personally, I would have much preferred objective, quantifiable metrics from which to base these bonuses, but we never quite pinned it down.

Executives – As it turned out our executive team did not have a bonus plan until our company sold to the Venture Firm that incorporated us into a legacy program they had for their other software company acquisitions. However, the plan consisted of a convoluted metrics formula multiplied by what appeared to be an arbitrarily assigned bonus factor. It was nearly impossible to track by any of the team and we each had to take it on blind faith that any distribution was accurate. But on that last point, the only executive bonus for which I participated actually turned out to be a calamity. The corporate headquarters at first announced that we hadn't qualified for the bonus, but once challenged a recalculation determined that we did indeed earn a sizeable bonus. Their formulation was so convoluted that even they couldn't figure it out. Not much of an incentive!

Prior to that acquisition, back in the 90's I had submitted an executive bonus plan to the Board that unfortunately was rejected. My executive bonus plan would have paid all our executives in the same manner – indexed to the performance of company objectives. I emphasize "all" executives because our majority owner thought it better to pay the VP of Sales independently upon attainment of sales quotas. Even though this is not an unique concept, I was diametrically opposed because:

1) promotion to an executive management level meant substantially higher compensation in exchange for a commitment to greater company goals, rather than individual department ones; and

2) a focus on singular department objectives worked against the cohesiveness of the team.

My plan was to generate the bonus pool from profits beyond our budgeted targets, both quarterly and annually, and distribute the accumulative amount equally among the executive team assuming we attained our objectives. The plan was weighted heavily toward profitability and the executive earn-out was quarterly as well as annually to assure attentiveness from the very start of the year.

As a final note, I truly desired to institute an ESOP (Employee Stock Option Plan), but got zero traction with the Board. I genuinely believe that when employees have an equity stake, no matter how small, they inherently acquire a heightened concern for the company. As example of this mindset transformation I have always pointed to the analogy of apartment renting versus homeownership. An employee stock option plan is perhaps the most salient ingredient in a compensation package, because if you really want an engaged work force, let them share in the company's ownership.

Now For The Details –
Starting With Sales

Well, having described my general approaches and philosophies for starting and sustaining a viable, meaningful startup business, it is now time to delve into the details of its most critical facets. Since I am most familiar with the Sales aspect, I'll start there. It will take several chapters to adequately cover this category. Let me begin with this chapter by explaining my background and experiences with sales.

My first actual exposure to selling was during my high school years while working in a Men's Clothing Store. Because the proprietor had no practical selling experience there wasn't any formal training, so my instincts were all I could rely on. Early on, I discovered that customers didn't much like the sales clerk lurking about ready to pounce at every touch of a wool suit fabric or silk accessory to persuade them it's the "perfect" item for them. Instead I learned that most customers preferred to know you were there to assist them, but otherwise allow them to browse until ready for greater engagement. It was, however, prudent to periodically check with the customer to invite questions and reinforce your readiness to help, but not at the frequency to be considered pestering.

I discovered as well that in order to assist (and sell) customers, I had to convey a confidence to them that I was capable. The best way to accomplish this was to dress the part or in other words "Dress for

Success". If a customer was going to trust that I could be their guide to contemporary fashion and accessory coordination, I had to both wear and be aware of current trends without being too flamboyant. This lesson is one I carried into my professional life – dressing appropriately for the audience I was intending to influence, be it prospects, customers, employees, vendors or partners.

I began my professional career as a computer System's Analyst, but quickly learned that the SA got all the "make-it-happen" work while the salesman did the wine-ing and dining, golfing and smoozing and not surprisingly, promising and giving, which didn't much look like work at all. And in those early days, the salesmen had unlimited expense accounts to make sure the "negotiating" was done well. That was all the inspiration I needed to decide Sales was where I belonged. Of course, no sooner had I made my move when companies made a paradigm shift in their treatment of Sales. Gone were unlimited expense accounts; implemented were more accountable reporting systems. But I soon learned I had a natural affinity for sales and I was hooked.

My professional sales career began when I accepted a trainee position in computer sales with the NCR (National Cash Register) Company at their Montgomery, AL branch office. NCR had a distinct sales method and in my first interview with the Branch Manager after my hire, he laid it out clearly for me. He said that if I followed the NCR sales plan he could assure me I would be successful, but if not, I was on my own. The broad steps of the plan in the order as NCR prescribed were:

The Introduction

The Survey

The Demonstration

The Proposal

The Close

I will expand each of these steps in upcoming chapters, but can tell you I faithfully followed this prescription and sure enough I found the success promised. During my two-year tenure as a junior sales rep, I contributed to the Montgomery Office's attainment as the Best-In-Class for their branch size category in each of those years. Following my Montgomery apprenticeship, I was offered a senior sales rep's position in Jackson, MS and willingly accepted, which led to the achievement in my second year as the nation's top computer sales representative and the prestigious honor of Director of the CPC (100 Point Club). Soon after, I was recruited by Unisys Corporation for a position in Sales Management. There I attained distinction in their Heavy Hitter's Club multiple times.

But sales of computer systems back then were a fickle phenomenon where the law of diminishing returns applied. One of the hazards of performing well in the attainment of sales targets, otherwise called quotas, is that management would consistently raise the bar every year to the point where it became more punishment than motivation. At the same time, technology was improving so quickly that, when I began my sales career, a computer sold for $1 million or more; ten years later they were selling for less than a tenth of those prices. Conversely, during the same time period computer horsepower was accelerating exponentially. That $1M computer's only function was payroll and the sales justification for making the investment was the replacement of manual labor – a roomful of payroll clerks. Ten years later the mini-computers did all the basic accounting, plus inventory, plus manufacturing, plus CAD/CAM and more. In essence, computers were getting more sophisticated and complicated while selling prices were falling precipitously and sales quotas were constantly growing, not a good trend line for a successful outcome. And it should be mentioned that although lower prices expanded the prospective client base and that may seem a positive, as it turned out it precipitated reduced sales territories and added personnel to attend them. Hence, it led to my final move in accepting the position with the Food Service Contract Company and leaving my place on the selling side of the desk for a seat on the buyer's side.

As an aside, I was always fascinated at what companies instigated as the solution to this dilemma of ever increasing sales quotas. When a top performer finally reached the tipping point and became disgruntled, they would immediately promote this individual into a sales management role in hopes of retention. However, the fallacy of this approach was:

1)   Removal of top sales producers from their most productive positions.
2)   Placement, frequently without training, in roles for which they may not be suited or qualified.

The result has almost always been diminished sales and a disrupted management process. But the solution has forever been as plain as the nose on our face – don't incessantly raise quotas. With a solution so obvious, why do companies continue this practice? I believe it occurs in top down management organizations where it's all about the numbers and a mentality of *"that's how it's always been done"*. Little heed is given to hearing from below and considering rational suggestions. This is the flaw that gives 'Learning Organizations' so great a competitive advantage. Fortunately for me, my acceptance of the Unisys offer included an 11 week formal sales management training regimen.

At this point, I do want to point out a significant twist in the above mentioned NCR Sales Plan. The Demonstration phase is actually out of place for the systems sales that we're chiefly addressing in this book. Actually, there are two types of demonstrations; one is included within the Survey phase while the primary Demonstration step is now positioned after the Proposal. Let me explain:

When NCR developed this Sales Plan they were "a" – excuse me – "The" Cash Register Company, selling physical registers store to store, often in rural areas off the back of a station wagon. Like computers these were tangible products that you could touch and feel. So, it was like selling vacuum cleaners door to door, once you assess the need (Survey), you demo the solution, and that's prior to divulging the terms (Proposal). But today's products are often concepts rather than hard goods, which are untouchable and considered non-tangible. So, for tangible products the Demonstration comes before the Proposal, while for non-tangible products it is positioned afterwards. For non-tangible products, like software, you may still perform a demonstration prior to your proposal, but it is a general overview of features and benefits with the purpose of inviting questions to help uncover needs. Consequently, I include this generic demonstration as part of and within the Survey phase. But the real Demonstration positioned after the Proposal is actually a proof of concept illustrating how the product will perform for the client and return the investment identified in the proposal. And this demonstration is likely much different than what might be assumed. Its most effective form is as a visit to a similar customer's site to show firsthand how the proposed concept made them successful.

From here I will expand each of these 5 selling steps as we explore their intricacies and application.

The Blind Leading The Deaf
– Sales Management Rant:

The entrepreneur, who seeded the evolution of our startup company was a man named Bill. He came from his humble beginnings selling food products out of his 1941 Chevy as a wagon-jobber. From there he grew an industrial food empire that included processing, manufacturing, distribution, retail and foodservice contracting, that at his passing, made his worth over $100 million. Bill was notoriously frugal, even to the extent of making note pads from the blank back side of used paper and chastising employees about their waste when finding paperclips on the floor. But there was one principle to which this penny-pincher was adamant: If you were in management, he was paying you to solve problems and manage – not type, file or make copies. He insisted that you delegate those activities to lower wage clerical or secretarial staff.

That's a principle I believe is relevant when it comes to the general practice of today's sales management. It has been my observation that sales and executive management put demands on their experienced sales team that perhaps makes management feel in control, but in reality only corrupts the productivity of the salespeople. What I'm getting at is management's insistence on salespeople documenting every sales contact, every sales call, every sales activity and every sales prediction. This insistence has become even more prevalent with the advent of sales database tools, such as SalesForce.com and others. What these tools have done is give management a false sense of security with the printing of pretty bar and pie charts with all manner of projections. Of course, the results presented by these projections are almost always erroneous and off base. Why? Because it depends upon individuals who are least equipped to perform the task accurately, have an intrinsic motivation to exaggerate and are most prone to fudge and mislead.

From my perspective this documentation demand places a burden on the sales team, making them less productive, performing an exercise that, in truth, generates distorted and sometimes worthless information. Let me explain:

1.   Good sales people are in general extroverts that enjoy human interactions and much prefer meeting with people versus sitting at a desk pounding away in solitude at a PC keyboard. From my experience the really good sales people loathe minutiae and will do it poorly.

2.   Sales people, if they're performing, should be tired by the end of their sales day and any updating of database information afterhours in their hotel room would be susceptible to mistakes. Besides, the outgoing sales person is likely more apt to be networking and/or socializing over dinner or other similar event afterhours. Others may well see afterhours as their private time for relaxing or engaging in other non-work activities.

3.   Assuming that a typical sales person will not choose to update their database information nightly means they will either perform the required task during precious daylight selling time or at some point on the weekend. If the former, the sales person will often account for the

lost daytime by inventing phantom sales calls and activities. If the latter, the sales person's recall may be faulty. Whichever alternative, information accuracy is compromised.

4.   As for management's requirement of assigning success percentages to the working prospect base, what it creates is an atmosphere in which the sales person is enticed to exaggerate probabilities. Has there ever been a good sales professional who wasn't overly optimistic about his/her sales closing chances? And how many sales managers would actually accept an underachieving forecast as an answer? Hence the graphical charts of pending sales are almost always inflated and imprecise.

5.   And finally, when the sales person's heart is not in it, results can be invalid. Although the advent of personal computers and digital assistants have now made typing a common task for everyone, not just clerical personnel anymore, there remains an aversion to the exercise when the activity isn't directly connected toward the desired end, in this instance a sale. And documentation to appease management's whim isn't a cause for an enthusiastic effort.

Now don't get the idea that I am totally against sales contact databases. I have always been a proponent of providing employees whatever reasonable tools they require to improve their productivity and performance. If a salesperson was one who would make good use of a sales contact database, I would willingly supply one. And I would be remiss to not mention that the sales contact database system had proved useful in managing other parts of our business, like our maintenance and support services or our contracts and billing administration. However, it was aptly applied post sale and orchestrated by accountants, technicians and administrators, individuals far better suited to contend with detail reporting.

And certainly, these contact database tools can be valuable in the right places. If the sales are targeted to individuals, like insurance or financial products, a sales contact database may be needed to keep up with the prospects' personal information and follow-up actions. My agent faithfully sends birthday greetings (although I consider it as much pandering as heartfelt) because the sales setting is more private. Our company's sales by comparison were to positions – foodservice director, administrator, chief financial officer – rather than just persons. Sure, they were individuals who occupied those positions, but they were mostly interested in how to improve their job performance and the operation of the facilities in which they were employed. So, there wasn't as much personal selling as conceptual selling. In that context, the contact database didn't have the same relevance.

I required a very simple process from our "experienced" sales representatives that helped me monitor our sales productivity and potential. Because our approach was consultative selling of software systems, it entailed a formal proposal to explain features and benefits, delineate responsibilities, and confirm prices. I only asked the sales team to provide a monthly spreadsheet showing outstanding proposals and sales closures, both successful and failed. With a quick glance I could determine whether a sales rep was working efficiently and/or effectively. If they didn't show enough new sales proposals, which I could audit from the file copies, I knew they weren't perhaps making enough sales calls or not properly qualifying their prospects. If their closing ratio wasn't strong enough, I could surmise that they weren't following the sales plan, calling on the right decision makers, capturing sufficient survey information, properly translating the value proposition, or skillfully completing the closing process. By scrutinizing these spreadsheets, I could immediately ascertain weaknesses and schedule counseling, assistance, education or discipline. And our one-on-one monthly review of these spreadsheets provided me with a much clearer picture of our true sales and revenue potential which I could then forecast throughout our financial reporting process.

You may have noticed that I mentioned my simple spreadsheet reporting was for "experienced" sales representatives. That's because trainees and rookies typically needed a greater management oversight to ensure they understood expectations and were sufficiently prepared to work independently. Therefore, they initially had greater reporting requirements beyond the spreadsheets.

The most salient argument I have heard for maintaining a sales contact database was to capture prospect information, cataloging names, positions, past activities and pending actions. Most often the argument was reinforced with a scenario of the sales territory transitioning to another representative, supposedly making it easier. But whenever a sales territory transition did occur, the common refrain heard from the new rep was that the information and facts within the database weren't accurate. And besides, other applications facilitated these same procedures for working prospects. We utilized Microsoft's Office, which included what became our primary communication method – Outlook email.

But what about preserving a database of potential, not current, prospects for our products? In our business we had access to an electronic subscription service called the "Healthcare Bluebook" whose premise was nothing more than renting a maintained database of all Healthcare accounts, including the management individuals within. While this service was considerably more economical than the shared contact database offerings, like SalesForce, I contend it was certainly more accurate as well. I am certain that like subscription databases are available for most every industry. In the upcoming chapter on Sales Prospecting, I will discuss even better methods for identifying, qualifying and approaching prospects. From my standpoint, I much preferred our sales professionals to spend their desk time preparing good proposals and reinforcing, primarily through email, our value proposition, not wasting valuable selling time uselessly replicating information in a futile database maintenance exercise.

As a final story that demonstrates one of the laws touted in the management theories of the Fifth Discipline, *"The harder you push, the harder the system pushes back".* It sums up sales management's typical naivety. This true story occurred while I was a budding salesman at NCR. As standard routine, the sales team (about 15 of us) would work in the office on Monday mornings completing call reports, filling out expense forms and preparing our week's activity schedules. As it happened, we were assigned a new Sales Manager (likely one of those untrained, high producing but disgruntled salesman promoted from another branch office) and to make a statement he decided the sales team should always be out making sales calls and never in the office, not even on Monday mornings. As a group we complied with his out-of-the-office edict and instead reconvened at the local Shoney's restaurant. What we understood was that prospects and customers didn't care to see salesmen on Monday mornings, as they too were organizing their weeks. Of course, our call reports from that point forward included false information of supposed sales calls during the wasted time having breakfast. And don't be fooled to think similar actions aren't taking place right under managements' noses today as well. It may not be breakfast at Shoney's, but it may be a secret round of golf or some other non-sales activity. The bottom-line is not necessarily what the salesperson is doing moment by moment, but rather are they engaged and primarily, are they closing ample business.

Good salespeople are an independent lot, not typically receptive to regimen. Management's best prescription for these go-getters is to:

- Engage them in the company's mission
- Advocate for their responsibility to the team
- Encourage them by conveying trust
- Monitor their progress and counsel when necessary
- Applaud their successes
- Reward them with creative compensation packages that hold their focus throughout the year.

I titled this Chapter "The Blind Leading the Deaf" because in my view, executives are blind to the reality of their sales database reporting process and sales personnel are deaf to management's demands and urgings to produce their perceived reality.

Step One – The Sales Introduction

Introduction sounds like a simple enough term, but in the sales game it is much more involved than might be assumed. There is preparation, prospecting, capturing attention, building rapport, qualifying and gaining approval to proceed.

Preparation – To be a successful sales professional, you have to invest in understanding both your business and your customer's business. Primarily, the textbooks teach that the three elements to this understanding are:

ü Product Knowledge

ü Industry Knowledge

ü Sales Knowledge

But I am compelled to add a fourth element, because it is so personal in my experience –

Communication Knowledge – A true sales professional must conquer the art of communication, both written and verbal. This hit home for me when I had to compose an introductory letter at the very start of my sales career. I had not been a model college student and failed to take seriously enough the repercussions of not applying myself in my English classes. And it came home to roost with this first introductory letter. Without exaggeration it took me two solid weeks to finish the single page letter. Like the sports interview with a vocabulary challenged student/athlete (perhaps minus the student part), I found myself often repeating words and phrases such as the athlete might repeat "you know". Remember that this was in the era before the PC, so my limited vocabulary caused me to constantly look up words in a hard copy dictionary to assure their proper meaning, but my poor spelling proficiency compounded my difficulty since I would often be searching for incorrectly spelled words. What I wouldn't have given for electronic Spell Check and Thesaurus! No salesperson today should have any excuse for not properly communicating with their prospects and customers.

Product Knowledge – To be a sales professional you must understand the capabilities of the product you are attempting to sell. More so, a sales professional must be able to translate (communicate) these capabilities, or features, of the product into the benefits for the customer. The key questions are: how will these features be applied to the customer's business and what are the expected results that improve their business? While product knowledge may not mean learning how to build or install the system you are selling, it does mean devoting the time and effort to learn your product thoroughly enough to creditably explain to the customer how they will recoup and profit from their investment in your system.

Industry Knowledge – This knowledge is multifaceted, in the respect that you have to understand the particulars of the industry(s) in which your product exists, the industry in which it will be employed and any subset of that industry within which your product will be applied. For instance, our company sold point-of-sale equipment and application software to the Healthcare Industry to be used by the Food & Nutrition Department. Therefore, we not only had to be cognizant of the POS and software industry practices, but we had to understand the processes, traditions and trends of Healthcare as well as the special intricacies of Food & Nutrition. Research, education and involvement are the prescription to gaining industry knowledge.

· Of course, the Internet is the preeminent tool for performing research on any subject. Staying current on your respective industries, operational best practices and projected future developments has become as easy as a mouse click. The Internet is also a great resource for discovering the philosophies and strategies of prospects you intend to target.

· Good resource channels for self-education include industry periodicals, organizational newsletters and textbooks whether hard copy or electronic media. Certainly, collaboration with your peers and customers is a splendid method for benchmarking concepts learned and accelerating your education process.

· Involvement is nothing more than learning by doing. Getting out there surveying prospects' operations, joining trade organizations, attending conferences and volunteering on association committees all prove valuable as learning exercises.

Sales Knowledge – some people think all that's needed to be a sales person is a friendly personality and a gift for gab. Nothing could be further from the truth, although those traits are advantageous. A sales professional must learn the strategies to the sales process and what steps in which order must be mastered to move the process along to a fruitful conclusion. Sales knowledge includes qualifying prospects, conducting supportive surveys and demonstrations, producing effective proposals, handling objections and closing sales, among many other needed skills.

Of course, success in sales, as in any professional position, requires general traits like dedication, diligence, persistence and time management. A successful sales professional makes their job look easy, but speaking from experience, there is much to master before that success comes.

Prospecting – The next step after proper preparation is prospecting. That term is simple enough and it basically means finding and cultivating prospective buyers for the product or service you offer. But the activities and actions to facilitate effective prospecting are not so simple.

In the old days (the 1970's) when I first began my sales career selling computer systems, prospecting consisted of acquiring membership lists from the state trade associations (manufacturers, hospital, etc.) or lists of top employers from local Chambers of Commerce, then hit the streets to do what we call "cold calling". Cold calling was the stopping in on targeted businesses to meet with a person of authority that could authorize the purchase of the product or service you were offering. When I started my career at NCR they still had a sales group selling mechanical cash registers and, in general, each salesman (and back then they were exclusively men) would drive from restaurant to restaurant cold calling and performing register demonstrations off the back of their station wagons.

As a member of the computer systems sales group, my cold calling consisted going door to door of businesses large enough to have or need automation. My typical MO was to stop in, mostly unannounced, and request a brief meeting with the President, Administrator, or other chief executive to introduce myself and my Company. And when I say brief, I mean under 15 minutes, often shorter so as to not abuse the privilege if granted the interview. Why the chief executive? Because any "mainframe" computer system purchase with its sizable investment would eventually land in the executive's office for approval. So why go through a long sales campaign only to discover that the executive vetoed it in the end.

The old adage is call high and broad – top executives to middle managers across the organization – if you hope to eventually make the sale of a large system purchase. I was fortunate to be selling in the Deep South where hospitality ruled the day. I sincerely doubt that I could have been as successful making unannounced cold calls in the Northeast section of the country where I was born and raised. Up North I likely would have needed pre-arranged appointments which would have required a different approach. But in Mississippi, I was granted a meeting about half the time even though I had dropped in unexpectedly. Sure, it took audacity to operate in this manner, but I assured myself that many chief executives appreciated my position, for if they themselves had not advanced through a sales role within their own organizations, they at least hoped their own sales or marketing forces were performing as aggressively for their respective businesses. Of course, these executives would always reference me to the individual within the organization responsible for making a computer purchase recommendation. And of course, whether I gained the appointment with the chief executive or not, my next call went to that responsible individual with an opening statement: *"Mr./Ms. (executive) suggested I follow up with you."* They, not knowing my relationship with the executive, naturally would open their doors with an apprehensive acceptance. My bold approach to cold calling helped me attain recognition as the nation's top computer salesperson for NCR in 1973.

But that was then and this is now and it's a new digital world. With the advent of the Internet, email, and social networks, the whole paradigm of prospecting has changed. Just prior to leaving Common CENTS Solutions, I had begun a project to make prospecting more productive and cost efficient. The premise was to build a more attractive, proactive, interactive and educational company web site and direct the sales team to encourage potential clients to investigate it. Rather than the Sales team traveling around the country "cold calling" prospects, our new model had the Sales team developing electronic campaigns to steer prospect eyeballs to our new web site. The following is the synopsis of our new prospecting game plan:

· Produce an updated more attractive web site with video clips, comprehensive yet easy to read content, and an abundance of customer testimonials, all serving as a tool to educate the visitor.

· Implement web site monitoring software that would measure visitors' interest based on their navigation and mouse clicks.

· Generate email marketing campaigns and blast them to prospects to induce them to visit our web site.

· Have the web site monitoring software score visitor interest and notify the appropriate salesperson when it exceeds our predetermined threshold.

· Have the salesperson follow-up with a phone call to arrange a physical meeting with those interested parties.

This new prospecting model certainly would drastically reduce the cost of sales by passively qualifying prospects and eliminating much of the traditional cold calling travel expenses. Conversely, the salesperson's productivity would increase considerably with a greater focus on prescreened, already interested parties. However, there is still room for the old, cold calling methodology. Once a salesperson had arranged a physical meeting with a pre-qualified web prospect, they could leverage that trip by conducting cold calls in that geographical vicinity.

And we certainly shouldn't forget some of the most practical prospecting venues – conventions and conferences. In the past, the salesperson's effort was devoted to convincing a potential prospect that our offering was worthwhile exploring during a five-minute conversation in a confined display booth. There was always marketing materials available as a takeaway, but the visitor ends up with so much material from other vendors that it's likely they might either overlook or ignore ours. If they do read the material, there wasn't a way for us to know. But with the new web site paradigm, the goal is to whet the booth visitor's interest enough to peruse the web site. They can certainly do that at any point during or after business hours, or perhaps on their smart phone immediately after leaving the booth. And if they do, the salesperson will know it and know also how great their interest is.

For sure it would be an injustice to not discuss the importance of social media in today's sales environment. Social media has become another venue to uncover prospects, but more so it is an excellent medium to foster relationships with real and potential customers. In the early days, trade publications were the best and perhaps only way to learn of customer and prospect accomplishments. And telephone was the mode for sharing tips and leads with industry peers. Granted I left the business before social media became so prevalent, but I can state some noteworthy observations:

· Social networking sites like Facebook and LinkedIn, among others, provide a convenient method for staying informed and in touch with many prospective client businesses.

· Today's executives seemingly don't much utilize social media. Perhaps the next generation of execs will.

· Many social media users are intermediate managers who have an affinity for communications and are most amenable to your exchanges. "Likes" and "endorsements" to their social media pages can gain you name recognition and acceptance with these clients.

· But not all are open to your interactions. Some prefer their privacy and would only be disturbed by too many placement attempts. Even though they have social media accounts, if they don't post much about themselves or update their activities regularly, they are likely not going to be receptive to your communications.

· Most of all it's not about you. It's not about what vacation you've been on or what you've done. It's all about the client and learning what awards and accomplishments they attained and acknowledging them with sincerity. It's about understanding how to gain their favorable opinion of you and your company and opening a dialog for a potential sale.

· Finally, social media may be great tools to share prospect leads and information with other vendors to which you have good relationships.

Ok, now that you've gotten an appointment with your prospect. What's your first concern? As the saying goes: 'first impressions last', so, gaining the prospect's favorable attention and building good rapport are chief objectives to get your sales scenario off to a positive start. In a word, genuineness is the key. You must present a professional, yet warm and friendly persona.

Gaining Favorable Attention & Building Rapport – There are several factors in order to make that good first impression and gain favorable attention with your prospect:

1) As we discussed earlier, certainly you have to dress appropriately for your audience. If you want to be taken seriously, you have to project that in your appearance. You want your prospect's reaction to be: "This appears to be an alert, successful individual. This person may have something of value to share. I will listen".

2) Introduce yourself and your company. And don't make the prospect have to ask for it again by promptly handing out your business card. More important than your name, be sure you speak the prospect's name. You might start with an opening like: "Mr./Ms. (*prospect name*), I'm (*your name*) with (*company name*). I appreciate this opportunity to share a few minutes of your time. I've heard many fine comments about your operation." Of course, you better be prepared to explain what those fine comments you've heard were. And don't denigrate your visit by saying something similar to: "I just happened to be in the neighborhood".

3) Speak distinctly and enthusiastically. Look your prospect warmly in the eye (but don't stare). Let your demeanor radiate how important this moment is to you. Your prospect will sense it may be an important experience as well. Remember too, before a prospect will buy your product or service, they must buy you.

4) You need to gage how much time is available for your appointment to determine what tact you should take in starting your conversation.

· If you have pre-set the appointment beforehand, with ample time, you have an opportunity to explore common interests you may have with your prospect. Take notice of any plaque, picture, certificate, etc. hanging on the wall or sitting on the desk. Maybe it's golf memorabilia, a family picture or civic club recognition. If you discover something in common – perhaps you're a Rotarian, have a similar family or play golf – you might offer a comment like: "I see you (_fill in the blanks_)", to engage a beginning conversation. While this conversation is off topic, it serves to ease the tension that seems always present at an initial meeting. But bear in mind, while you and he/she may relish a discussion of a common passion outside the business, it isn't your reason for the meeting so don't belabor it. Keep it brief and proceed to your business purpose.

· If you have been granted an ad-hoc interview as a result of a cold call, there isn't time for the niceties, so it's imperative you get straight to the point. If your prospect seems receptive at the end of your introductory meeting, you may have an opening to mention an observed common interest. But you will need to rely on your wits for its appropriateness.

5) In terms of the crux of your introductory conversation – your business purpose for being there – plan your opening statement to immediately capture your prospect's attention. Here's an example of an opening script we might have used in our Common CENTS Solutions business:

"Mr./Ms. (*prospect name*) I'm here today to familiarize you with our automated system for your Food & Nutrition Department that has been proven in other hospitals to measurably improve patient satisfaction while it reduces food cost enough to repay the investment." "For instance, (*customer name*) moved their patient satisfaction scores from the 70's into the 90 percentiles and reduced their food cost by 20%, which not only improved their image, it produced a return on their investment of just 18 months."

From this point you can anticipate that your opening statements have spiked your prospect's curiosity enough to ask the 'How' question, which happily moves the conservation to a more explanatory level. Naturally, your script has to be structured to fit your particular product or service. And as you likely noticed, name dropping is a good strategy. To the prospect there is safety in numbers and/or recognizable colleagues that have adopted the proposition you prescribe. My script's second statement could have just as easily said: "You may not be aware that more than 28 hospitals similar to yours have implemented our solution in the past year."

6) So, where does this introductory conversation lead and to what end? Our end game for this first meeting is to get a reading on how really interested your prospect is and to move your sales plan toward the next step – The Survey. This is called qualifying. To qualify or measure interest, your prospect has to agree to take some action. Obviously, we want the prospect to agree to let you perform a review of their business (The Survey). However, if you sense a significant resistance to the more

intrusive survey, the alternative would be to request time for a presentation (the survey demo mentioned earlier) Therefore, your final question might take the form of:

> · "Mr./Ms. (*prospect name*) we would relish the opportunity to perform a survey (or presentation) for you to determine if we can bring your facility the same fantastic results as our other customers. Do you agree?

But even if this first meeting proves premature for agreement to conduct the survey or presentation, you can still qualify your prospect by obligating them to do something. Perhaps it's their commitment to peruse your website, or contact one of your customers (one you recommend), or schedule a second meeting. In every case, make sure you have included an agreement that you will follow-up with an action (phone call, meeting, etc.) in a specified time frame (2 weeks, 6 months, etc.). Your purpose is to answer evolving questions, gage continued interest and confirm next steps.

7) As you might surmise, you know you have a qualified (interested) prospect if they agree to invest either their time or their money. THIS IS THE MOST IMPORTANT POINT IF YOU PLAN TO BE SUCCESSFUL IN SALES. Every contact with your prospect should end with you qualifying them as you move them along in your sales process. Each meeting must end with you asking for the prospect to commit their time (or their staff's) to an exercise, like participating in your survey, OR their money, like signing your contract, OR both, like attending a seminar at your office.

8) Some sales gurus have suggested you can obligate your prospect by presenting them with some type of gift handout in initial meetings. I conversely, do not advocate this suggestion. To begin, I believe it cheapens your product or service by sending the message that you need to curry favor in order to get their business. That your offering is not beneficial enough to stand on its own. Secondly, if the gift is of token quality (a pen, golf tees, etc.), it is likely nothing more than a trinket to the prospect. A more substantial gift could be misinterpreted as more bribe than present. Besides many businesses and organizations now have ethics' policies limiting gift values. But having stated my objection to arbitrary gift giving, I can say there are occasions when a meaningful souvenir may be appropriate. Primarily these are occasions where a heartfelt thank you is de rigueur. For instance, I had several Healthcare Food & Nutrition Directors dedicate themselves and members of their staff to a customer site visit that required travel and an overnight stay. To say thank you and to leave them with a keepsake of their visit, I provided each participant a unique cookbook. And it so happens, that the cookbook was authored by the chef and director of the facility we visited. Not only did we secure good business as a result of the visit, we left a vivid remembrance with those who have yet to decide, and we provided some reward and good will with our customer for hosting our visit.

9) Postscript – This post is about building rapport with your prospect, but that may reference more than the decision makers. Don't forget about the administrative assistants. It is always advantageous to get favorable reaction from these gate keepers. To make my point, I

recently read, on the 50th anniversary of JFK's assassination, about how Life Magazine's bureau chief exclusively acquired the Zapruder film of the event. Of course, there were many organizations clamoring for the film, but during the aggressive bidding war process for the film, this bureau chief took time with Zapruder's assistant, discovered she was from Illinois as was he, found high school basketball as a common subject of interest and in a short time became like old friends. While his gentlemanly approach to Zapruder, his commitment to not exploit the film and his bid price were all important factors, he attributed his rapport with Zapruder's assistant as the one that may have tipped the scale in his success.

Qualifying – Aside from the critically important requisite of qualifying the prospect's real interest at each contact point along the sales process by their willingness to commit time or monetary resources, there is a good deal more to qualifying that remains within the salesperson's domain.

There is a fundamental qualifying process for which every salesperson should be aware, before they ever position themselves to ask for their prospect's order commitment. These are qualifying items for the salesperson to determine rather than an action by the prospect. These items differentiate a "suspect" (one that could perhaps be a candidate for your product or service) from a bona-fide "prospect" (one that could definitely buy your product or service) Here are the basic qualifying questions a salesperson must answer during the Introduction phase of the sales process:

1. *Does this organization/individual need my product or service?* – Often this determination can be made long before the sales approach with some background investigation. For instance, an application we offered at Common CENTS Solutions was a hotel-style, room service meal delivery system for hospital patients, and while appropriate in the Acute Care Hospital setting, it certainly had no fit in a Psychological Hospital where patients, for obvious reasons, did not have the liberty to place their own mealtime food orders.

Of course, often you may not be able to predetermine a need. Therefore, it may mean exploring for that answer during your initial approach sales call. Groping for specific needs while presenting interesting appeals during the sales call can certainly be difficult, but the way forward is simply to ask. In our case, my initial question may have been: "Do you currently have room service for your patients?" If the answer was yes, then the follow-up would have been an open ended "How is that working for you?" And depending upon that response another may be "Are you seeing cost savings along with improved patient satisfaction?" And afterwards "Can you tell me more?" In this interview session my third question is somewhat of a trap question. One of the most salient benefits of our room service application was the innovative manner in which we managed the labor involved in executing the meal delivery, whereas our competition required excessive cost to provide the same. Hence, this third question was a lead in to explain an advantage that could have relevance to the prospect. Now if the answer to my initial question happened to be a no rather than yes, then my follow-up may have started with "Have you investigated this possibility and what are your feelings about patient room service?" This would leave an opening to briefly explain the benefits of our room service system and gauge both interest and need.

2. Does the organization/individual have the ability to buy my product or service? – Regardless of the need or interest in your product or service, a prospect must have the financial resources to afford your offering. This determination may be as straightforward as a credit check or may take exploratory questions into budgeting, financial stability and cash reserves. In my practice, hospitals of the size we targeted were nearly all stable financially and had well defined budgeting processes, so my primary determination was to learn if the Food and Nutrition Department had an approved budget allocating enough resources to fund my project. Naturally, it was always best to be involved beforehand to help arrange that budget approval if possible.

3. Does the organization/individual have the authority to buy my product or service? – Basically, the question here is 'Am I calling on the right person(s) and location'? Sales time is precious and it needs to be productive. Calling on individuals that are not decision-makers means wasting an opportunity to move the sales process toward a close. In today's world of consolidations and acquisitions buying decisions are often made at centralized offices or corporate headquarters. Calling on remote offices or branches without anyone with buying or recommending authority means you're marching in place rather than moving forward. But if you're unfamiliar with a large corporate organizational chart it may be worth your while to meet with someone with recommendation influence that can also help you ascertain the corporation's chain of command and who the actual decision-makers are.

In my work situation I had an extremely large hospital corporation with 8 regional districts consisting of multiple hospitals within each region's geographically area. So, my sales strategy was to cover all the bases. Most importantly was to create a relationship with the ultimate decision makers at the home office; secondly it was important to gain the endorsement of the technical recommenders in the regional offices; finally, it required the education of the food & nutrition directors in the individual hospitals. Certainly, making sales calls to individuals in the HQ and regional offices was easy enough to imagine, but how do you educate 200+ individual hospitals without dedicating your entire sales time to the project? The answer was to conduct regional seminars and attend national as well as the corporation's own private vendor fairs. Covering all the bases was essential to capture their business and secure it in future years.

Of course, the bottom line of the Approach phase is to find and develop valid prospects and gain their approval to proceed to the Survey phase. As I will discuss, the survey is the real fact-finding exercise that allows you to substantiate the prospect's needs and build a justification for the investment in your product or service.

Now once you've answered these above qualifying questions for yourself, made your initial sales approach with the viable prospects you've uncovered and qualified those prospects by their commitment to go forward, you can categorize them. I've seen a myriad array of schemas for categorizing prospects, but for me, I had a process as easy as A, B, C.

'A' was for <u>active</u> prospects. The sales plan dictated the what and when for the next activity. These prospects indicated a need for the product or service and had the financial resources allocated to funding it. These prospects also held the highest priority for sales time because typically there was immediacy to their closing.

'B' was for <u>budding</u> prospects. These prospects indicated a definite need for the product or service, but either hadn't budgeted for its acquisition or approved the release of its funding. These prospects required routine follow-up contact and fortification of the value proposition to build toward the purchase of the product or service. In the past this meant both phone and face to face contact periodically, but with today's social media technology staying in touch has become much more reasonable and efficient. I would routinely find reasons (relevant news, helpful tips, new customer announcements, etc.) to communicate with my B level prospects and always ended my emails with a reinforcement of some benefit my system would hold for the prospect. The intent of this follow-up of course, was to assure I and my product or service were top-of-mind when the funding for the project was finally authorized and to be ready to pursue the sale to a close with this newly active prospect.

'C' is for <u>could be</u> prospects. These suspects have potential for moving up to the B level but not immediately, so it is important to stay in touch, but only sporadically. These are potential prospects that I might touch base with two to six times a year, often at trade shows or through email marketing blasts.

Let the Real Selling Begin
– The Survey

So you've qualified the prospect and they have agreed to invest their organization's time to let you perform a survey of their operation. This is the next logical step after the Introduction when following the strategic sales plan. The Survey is not only a fact-finding mission, but it's your prime opportunity to educate and sell the prospect on your company, your product and/or service, and most importantly you.

When I began my sales career with mainframe computers in the 70's, the survey phase would typically take upwards to 6 months or more to complete. When I ended my career as a software application provider, the survey could be accomplished in as little as a two-hour slideshow presentation or webinar. But both were aimed at the same objective – to discover the prospects' needs, uncover weaknesses in their current systems, and explore for unique advantages my system could offer them.

In the earlier mainframe days, the survey devoted much time determining capacities, speeds, reliabilities, application requirements and direct cost savings. Much was the same while selling Point-Of-Sale systems, but it also included ease of use, security and cost of ownership. In the latter application software era, the focus was more on operating features, the benefits each feature could provide and the return on the investment. In any case, the fact-finding mission was the same. It may have been a series of detailed questions from a multipage survey guide in those early days, or simple open-ended questions ("how do you handle that?") when you sensed interest during a present-day presentation. The goal, of course, was to gather enough vital information in order to summarize your system's value in a sales proposal.

A product demonstration was often included during the survey phase to showcase your system's features and help explain how it might benefit the prospect. I emphasize that in any conversation during this Survey phase, especially during the demo, it is most important to translate any feature you tout into the real benefit to the prospect. This product demo is different than the Demonstration I referenced as one of the formal steps in the sales plan and that which follows the Proposal step. The Demonstration step of the sales process is a "proof of concept" demo and will be discussed subsequently.

This Survey phase is your best selling opportunity because:
1. You already know that the prospect perceives a need to improve since they have agreed to commit their time to the survey.

2. If you qualified the prospect correctly, you will have attentive listeners.

3. As you discover weaknesses in their current operation, you have the opening to explain how your product/service can cure them.

4. As you learn the details of their operation, you can flaunt certain unique features (benefits) of your product/service that a competitor cannot replicate.

5. You have this occasion to gain audiences with the decision makers and the most influential recommenders.

In regards to point #5, I must emphasize that getting access to these individuals is likely a critical factor in bringing your sales campaign to a successful close. The survey forms I used in the 70's included conversations with all the top echelon of the prospect's management team. In more recent times, I was adamant about the attendance of upper management in any presentation I would make to a prospect's organization.

Once you have enough knowledge you then can proceed to the Proposal phase of the sales plan. However, it is imperative that you not go forward if you haven't gathered all the appropriate information to completely understand the value your product and/or service will provide the prospect. You should follow-up as often as necessary until you have adequate answers in order to compose a compelling argument for implementation of your solution.

Get To The Finish Line
– Proposal, Demonstration & Close

Once the Survey has been completed, you can proceed to securing your new customer. I have grouped the three remaining steps of the sales process together because if you've completed the first two steps – Introduction and Survey – properly these activities should occur within a close proximity to each other.

The Proposal: In the early days of my sales career, proposals could have been judged by their weight. They often were so stuffed with boilerplate fluff that they had to be assembled in 3-inch binders and sometimes multiple binders. This even remained the case decades later for proposals generated by the Food Service Contractor's sales team. However, at Common CENTS Solutions, we found a more streamlined proposal, perhaps 10 to 20 pages, proved noticeably more effective. Those historical hefty proposals generally included sections for a cover page, review letter, executive summary, company history, promotional material, hardware specs, software specs, support and service policies, customer user lists, disclaimers, investment overview, and implementation schedule. Much of it was nonessential filler creating way too much reading for decision makers and causing them difficulty in zeroing in on the most relevant sections.

Our typical proposal at Common CENTS Solutions consisted generally of an executive summary, a detailed investment synopsis and a sample contract.

1) The executive summary should be intentionally brief and to the point, usually condensed to a single page. It summarized the true benefits of the proposed solution and I insisted each of ours include the 3 to 5 foremost advantages for choosing our solution over the competitors'. By major advantages I am not referencing features of the system, but rather how our features will improve the client's operation and results, our real benefits. Examples may have been the 10% increase in cafeteria profits from the elimination of mistakes and theft because of our POS controls; the 20% improvement in service speed and revenues through our cashless program; the dramatic rise in patient satisfaction, the food cost reductions and the labor productivity advances facilitated by our room service application. Further, these examples should ideally translate into hard dollars or numbers based on the clients actual operating volumes and statistics. For instance: $125,000 gain in cafeteria profits from POS control, 4 more customers per minute plus $250,000 sales increase with half going to profit from cashless, and customer satisfaction into the 90 percentiles and food cost savings of $50,000 from room service. Add to this the substantiation for all the labor productivity improvements and you have an extremely compelling proposal case.

2) For the investment synopsis we used a fill-in-the-blanks automated spreadsheet program. Once we entered the pertinent factors (# of apps, terminals, users, etc.) the pages populated with the correct pricing and extensions. It also filled in our pre-formulated estimates for implementation hours and costs. Our spreadsheet cover sheet congregated all the chief components into grand totals. Included on this

sheet were any of our disclaimers, such as proposal expiration period, customer obligations and other contingencies. Most importantly our investment synopsis had a prominent section that estimated the customer's return on investment (ROI) in terms of months. This was based upon the client's operating volumes captured during the Survey stage. Once that ROI period expired, the customer would then reap the profits unimpeded. This enabled the decision makers to quickly assess the investment / value proposition, making it easier to approve our offer.

3) The inclusion of the sample contract is intended to expedite its approval and conclude with the customer's signature. Every sale requires a contract negotiation process, sometimes quite lengthy. The sample contract accomplished two objectives: To begin it sent a clear signal to the client that we expected to acquire their business. And secondly, it provided us an avenue to continually follow-up, as well as benchmark the prospect's seriousness to begin the relationship with our company. If the client showed hesitation in negotiating the contract terms, it was a cue to us that perhaps they were not sold on our value proposition and essential for us to revisit our proposal with them to reinforce its benefits.

The Demonstration: At times the presentation of the proposal is enough to consummate the sale, but often, especially if what you're selling is an intangible like software, it will require a proof of concept. This is what I call the Demonstration phase. Now there may be actions conducted during the Survey phase that we call product demonstrations, but their purpose is to facilitate the discovery of a client's operating weaknesses by showing system features and getting feedback on how these features might improve their process. This Demonstration phase generally serves to validate the valuable features and benefits uncovered in the Survey and highlighted by the Proposal. While this demonstration could be conducted in a neutral office environment, it is much more credible if conducted at a current customer's site. Of course, the customer should be one that represents the same systems as proposed to the client and one that is well satisfied with your company's performance. You are also well advised to make certain the customer is familiar with the prospect's goals, expectations and concerns. And don't panic if there is a support "war story" or two that your customer is likely to tell because it only serves to authenticate them as real and not a setup. Of course, that does assume that any support issue was promptly and properly dispatched to the satisfaction of this customer.

The Close: Securing the order is a natural and seamless progression, provided you have correctly qualified the prospect starting at your Introduction, educated and encouraged them throughout the Survey, persuaded them with a compelling Proposal, and perhaps corroborated your proposal projections with an undeniable Demonstration. There may be some eleventh-hour questions (most often referred to as objections) that might need to be addressed, but once the client has been reassured, asking for the order should be stress-free. This is a reminder as well that you needn't necessarily wait until all the steps of the Sales Process are complete to ask for the order. At any time during the process, particularly after the Proposal presentation you can ask for the customer's business. These typically are called trial closes and may be attempted when the prospect conveys a distinct signal that they have intent to buy.

And speaking of objections, when I was in my early computer sales training, I recall a full day's session of nothing more than handling objections. This session stressed programmed responses to the most common prospect objections like "I'll think it over" or "your price is too high". And as the dutiful new salesman, I tried them all. But they seemed so forced and disingenuous, as if I were trying to just con the prospect rather than the prospect being convinced. If you have followed the full sales plan appropriately, any objections at this point will naturally be seen as a prospect's final concerns or a last chance negotiation tactic.

Keeping a cool head and discussing the prospect's objections openly will certainly produce your desired result, the sale. The most common objective I've experienced in my sales career was the 'price too high' criticism, but only rarely was this objection sincere. Unsurprisingly, this is usually the prospect's attempt to get their best deal possible, but too, it may be a very clear signal the prospect intends to buy your system or service. And there are a couple of methods I used to address this predictable event:

One is a maneuver used universally in the sales realm – a fallback price position. You are likely familiar with automobile pricing policies whereas the car dealer has a sticker price and a bottom-line selling price, and depending upon your negotiation skill, you will typically pay a price somewhere in between. Well that was the methodology used in my early selling days and what we sometimes turned to toward the end of my tenure at Common CENTS Solutions.

My approach during my successful computer sales days was to offer a published manufacturers list price, but retain a fallback discounted price to unveil if needed. Since I was selling competitive computers against the big blue juggernaut, IBM, in the 70's, I would absolutely never divulge my price until I presented my proposal. My standard response would always be "I can't know what my price will be until I complete the survey to determine the configuration details". Then I would perform my comparisons of like features, components, capacities and speeds, leaving the prospect to mentally attach the IBM pricing for such capabilities. Unquestionably, IBM was always the highest price system on the market during that period in history, so when, finally, I would expose my suggested manufacturers pricing in the proposal, it was an attention grabber at a customary 20% investment savings. Of course, IBM was formidable even at their higher price, so if I sensed the prospect was wavering, I might offer a limited time additional discount (netting pricing between my proposal and fallback) to push them over the finish line.

And speaking of IBM and keeping a cool head during the final negotiations, let me relate a real case study to consider. I was involved in the possible sale of a Unisys computer system to replace IBM at a longtime customer. We were down to the final meetings, which consisted of the prospect's morning conference at IBM's local office before an afternoon meeting at our branch office. We had proven our value during our systems comparisons and felt confident we would win the day. However, when our meeting was in mid-stream, the prospect began to throw up several novel objections, mostly involving future capacities or features unique to the IBM system. After several panicky minutes on the defensive trying to technically address their supposed concerns, I recovered my senses enough to stop the conversation. Then I simply asked this question: Are you really ever going to need these features or are these just ploys by our competitor to fuzzy up your decision? The prospect took a minute to contemplate the question before clearly recognizing the ploy and within the next 15 minutes we had their order and a new customer.

The other method I utilized to address the prospect's "your price is too high" objection was to stand my ground and not discount at all. This was my policy during the formidable startup years at Common CENTS Solutions, Inc. As you may remember from an earlier chapter, we intentionally positioned our initial product pricing at about 20% below our main competitor's price. We took this approach in order to build a customer base faster from which we could prove our product's performance and reliability. Once accomplished, we could raise our prices accordingly. The only limited discounting we allowed was for volume purchasing. We structured our operating costs to match our anticipated revenues leaving some for a sensible profit. So whenever this "price too high" objection arose, I would look the prospect straight in the eye and state that we had priced our products and services fairly, arranged our support to meet the quality they expected and retained a reasonable profit in order to sustain our business at these high standards. Further I could honestly tell them that the price offered to them was the same as offered to all our other customers and to provide them a reduced price would be unfair to those customers. This strategy worked surprisingly well and price was never the reason for losing a sale. And our company grew at a remarkable rate, becoming one of our State's fastest growing companies several times.

However, once we were acquired by the first venture firm, this strategy was abandoned. These new venture partners insisted on sales above all else, sanctioning discounting so severe that sometimes it obliterated the profitability from the sale. (*Look for my rant on venture partners in an upcoming chapter.*) This new pricing approach along with other partner enforced policies had the effect of devaluing the perception of our products and eventually led to a dearth in sales and the auctioning of our company to a second venture firm. Fortunately, we were able to retake possession of our pricing strategy, although too late to return to the no discount policy, and we morphed it into a restricted range of allowable discounts within a salesperson's authority. And too, we regained our sales momentum.

Regardless of your pricing strategy you have to offer a product or service of value and back it up with worthy support. Do that and you can be successful as a salesperson and a company. What I trust you can extrapolate from any of these related experiences above is: If you follow the Sales Plan faithfully through the Introduction, Survey, Proposal, Demonstration and Close, you will know your client intimately, recognize the advantages they will reap from your product or service, illustrate those rewards effectively to them and rest comfortably with the assurance they will soon become your customer.

Do You See What I See?
– A Metrics Rant

Well I've held it in about as long as I could, so for this chapter I've chosen to give my perspective on perhaps the most revered practice in operational management – performance metrics. Wikipedia explains that a performance metric should support a range of stakeholder needs from shareholders to employees and customers. But all too often, in my experience, performance metrics were focused exclusively on the shorter-term financial aspects of the business, mostly cost controls. Rarely have the companies or owners I have worked for considered customer value or employee satisfaction. And most times these metrics are developed as a one size fits all without regard to specific circumstances of individual operations or locations. I consider them "lazy" metrics, because they have been established without an effort to evaluate unique conditions that may make them more detrimental than helpful in certain situations. The following is an historical list of examples and outcomes of foolish metrics I have experienced with organizations for which I have worked:

The NCR Corporation – While working in Mississippi in the early 70's as an Account Manager for NCR, the edict was sent down from national headquarters that service technician staffing for the computer division would be determined as a factor (metric) of maintenance revenue per tech. Accordingly, the accountants used a highly profitable branch as their model and as was told to me, it was the New York City branch located in the Empire State Building. Of course, it was easy to envision lofty maintenance revenue parameters per technician in that environment where attending service calls meant simply getting on and off an elevator at different floors. However, in Mississippi we had customers spread across the state in our population centers, which generally were over an hour's drive from our city of Jackson branch office. Certainly, our situation required a tweaking of this universally decreed metric to accommodate our dead time traveling from city to city. Yet that was never a consideration. These were the times of mainframe computers and Big Blue IBM. We had made significant inroads in acquiring computer customers for NCR in Mississippi, but once our service response suffered as a result of this metric, so did our attrition and sales.

Valley Food Service, Inc. – In the 80's I was employed by this food service contractor. I was new to the food service industry so came in with no preconceived notions. One metric that was ingrained throughout the operating division was the management of food cost at 40% of revenue. But this was a transitional time in the institutional food service industry to a more hospitality and retail orientation, which meant better quality menu offerings in order to stay competitive. But this 40% mentality was so ingrained that it was nearly impossible for the company to upgrade their menu. There was little consideration for the sales increases (and profits) that would likely transpire from upscaled menu choices. In fact, I recall an instance where a creative hospital food service manager began offering a popular "steak night" once a month. Instead of serving a typical beef entrée for $4.99 with perhaps a $2.00 (40%) food cost, she served a $6.99 ribeye that might have cost $3.50 (50% food cost). Her district manager from the corporate office took her to task for her inflated food cost, never recognizing the popularity or profitability (an extra 50 cents) of her idea. What concerned the district manager most was his grading on the food cost metric come bonus time. Lost in his and the company's thinking were customer and employee satisfaction, as well as profitability. Certainly, this ridged thinking abdicated many potential corporate clients to the more progressive competition.

Tenax Company: By the early 2000's, Common CENTS Solutions had become a viable operating company spun off from Valley Food Services when Valley's Board decided to divest itself of it. Hence my first encounter with a venture firm, the Tenax Company. Tenax was primarily a local entity funded by a retired executive who accumulated sizeable wealth from an IPO of a company for which he served as CEO. This experience was an awakening for me to the evils of venture companies (reference venture capital rant chapter). Needless to say, some ill conceived directives from the venture partners led to a slowdown in our business which in turn led to the hiring of the infamous consultant company (50% owned, of course, by the venture partners). After months analyzing our business, at ample expense, they produced in my opinion the most egregious representation of metrics use. In this case, they produced the antithesis of the "lazy" metrics; they did the consultants' typical textbook overload in order to justify their $50,000 fee. While extensive, it was too elaborate to be practical. Regarding sales, for instance, these consultants recommended that our sales professionals would be compensated according to their performance of over 100 metric items, including recruitment of personnel and speeches to organizations. And bonuses and/or commissions would be paid once a year after the grading of metrics accomplishment. Now having earned my stripes in sales, I can assure you that the successful sales professional abhors superfluous distractions and looks for commission gratification as close to the action as is feasible. Their focus should basically be: generate leads, develop prospects and close profitable business, and compensation should be paid immediately once the new business is secured. Other functions (certainly not 100) important to the organization should simply be added to their job description for evaluation of the salesperson's overall performance in consideration of raises and/or promotions.

Constellation Software, Inc.: Once the Tenax partners recognized they were out of their element, although still unable to resist micromanaging the decision-making, they decided to entertain the advances of a much larger venture group, Constellation Software. This consummated in the acquisition purchase of Common CENTS Solutions by this Canadian firm in 2009. Constellation began as a company selling software applications in the golf country club market. They were successful enough to capture a majority market share, leaving acquisition as their best route to growth. From the takeover of competing software companies in their industry, they diversified into other markets with acquisition targets exclusively in the business of designing and selling software. We were apparently their first acquisition that sold significant hardware (point-of-sale networks). This became abundantly clear to me with my first financial report post acquisition. The report was missing all revenues from our hardware sales, which represented about a third of our business. Naturally we followed-up with Corporate Accounting to correct their omission. Their explanation: "ours was the first company with a hardware component". What we couldn't get them to correct was their mainstay operating metric: revenue based payroll headcount. Evidently, in their beginning as a solo software company, they had developed a formula for the ideal staffing to support their systems and they carried this prescription forward as they acquired other software firms. Perhaps this formula can apply when it's all software, but when you introduce the hardware element into the mix, there has to be an adjustment. Software can remotely be supported, maintained, upgraded and even installed electronically without ever leaving the office. Hardware, however, often requires personnel on site to install or repair. And this logically may necessitate added manpower in comparison to pure software. But that adjustment wasn't even a topic for discussion, and as I understand after my departure, this enforced metric overtaxed employees, undermined service, disappointed customers and lost business. For the two years after the takeover that I remained involved, it also cost us money. The reason was because compliance with this restrictive headcount metric facilitated the expense of more off the payroll, outside contractors to provide the services that customers deserved. This one-size-fits-all headcount mentality was flawed and would have taken just a little rational thinking to design the right headcount metric for our individual environment. This was a symbolic example of what I term a "lazy metric."

But please don't assume from this rant that I am anti metrics. I am wholeheartedly for metrics that are well conceived, conform to the company culture, and promote the values and mission of the enterprise. Financial metrics can certainly play a part, but can't be the only focus.

Think of metrics development like the changes that occurred in major league baseball as represented in the Brad Pitt movie 'Moneyball'. Using technology to parse player statistics geared to his team's unique needs, he was able to staff his roster with players that didn't fit the standard profile demanded by all the others... and it proved to be a winning formula. No more lazy metrics; do the work.

Corporations Are People Too... NOT – A Venture Capital Rant

"Corporations are people too" was the statement that doomed Mitt Romney's 2012 campaign for President of the United States, because it seemed an insensitive preference for business over the public welfare. The same may be said of Venture Capital Firms penchant for profits over the best interest of customers and employees.

Ok, I've been told my "rants" don't really qualify as such because there isn't enough anger. I suppose I've mellowed over the years. So, let's call this my strong opinion about the evils of Venture Capital Firms. And please don't get the idea that I'm a cynic, because certainly I am not. I am the ultimate optimist. I couldn't have been an exceptional salesperson unless I was unconditionally optimistic. But I am a realist as well and this rant, excuse me – strong opinion, comes from my firsthand experiences and other observations.

Let me start by telling you about my impression of one of my favorite TV programs, Shark Tank. On this show budding entrepreneurs present their business ideas to five individual investor "sharks", seeking capital and expertise to help grow their businesses. In exchange the entrepreneurs offer a percentage of their equity. The sharks evaluate these opportunities and on those that they perceive offer a good return for their investment, bid against each other by negotiating investment deals with the entrepreneurs. With the exception of one, nicknamed Mr. Wonderful, these sharks seem genuinely interested in helping these entrepreneurs if their ideas are worthy. Perhaps it is my optimism, but the sharks appear to want nothing more than to provide the needed capital, help with important sales contacts, and offer their advice and wisdom, leaving the actual decision-making and authority to the entrepreneurs. Mr. Wonderful conversely seems only to want what's best for him, disregarding the best interests of the entrepreneurs or their potential customers. He gives the impression that money in his pocket is more important than product quality, pricing fairness, or entrepreneur autonomy. It is Mr. Wonderful's ostensible greed that parallels my experience with Venture Firms.

My first experience was the transfer of ownership from our original parent company Valley Food Service to the venture firm Tenax. At first, my optimism for this relationship was high because the Tenax owners were local residents and former executives with sizable corporations. And during the acquisition they spoke of remaining in the background allowing our company to continue on its successful track, offering advice and appraisals only during monthly board meetings. Unfortunately, it was only a few months into the new partnership before these partners began to undermine the process – introducing "friends" into the business for fabricated upper management positions. Despite these distractions we continued to grow, launching our innovative patient room service application soon thereafter.

As with any newly launched product, a support infrastructure is the first call to order and for an innovative application like ours, the learning curve takes some time. While our sales team was selling our system, we were hiring and training staff to shore up our support team. Thankfully the popularity of our system created a backlog of orders to be installed, indeed a good problem to have. To make sure this new room service system was implemented correctly and the service personnel properly prepared, we scheduled our implementations about every other week, allowing the in-between weeks for readying upcoming installs and following-up with previous weeks' installs. Once we had an expanded and competent implementation support team in place, we planned to accelerate our installations to every week with even multiple installs overlapping at times. However, the best laid plans of mice and men.........

Once these venture (or is it vulture) partners noticed the worth of our backlog, dollar signs glazed over their eyes and despite my strong objections, they forced an accelerated installation timetable. It appeared obvious to me that in their naivety they thought they could churn the cash inflow faster bringing more profits for dividend payments at year's end. Unfortunately, instead they killed the goose that lays the golden egg. These owners had accounting backgrounds and worked in the chemical and shipbuilding industries as CFO and CEO respectively. They had never worked closely in the technology sector. They failed to recognize the time and resources required to prepare and complete a successful implementation of a software system as complex as ours. Because we didn't have the conventional infrastructure ready, we were running a pattern whereas the installation teams weren't afforded the time to properly prepare, attempted to make up for it on the fly at the customer's site, and had to abandon the installation prematurely before the software was fully implemented. It was no mystery why our customers became disillusioned and disgruntled. Soon the word circulated that Common CENTS Solutions may have had best-of-breed applications but its support was so severely lacking that it was not a satisfactory customer experience. And as you may have guessed our sales quickly dissipated as well.

At this point for the next year or so, two actions orchestrated by the Tenax owners were particularly confounding and disheartening. First, while we were suffering an off year, they directed we would hold a combined planning meeting with a Tenax owned sister company, sharing the cost. While this may not seem so strange on the surface, what made it so unsettling was that it was arranged to be held at a sportsman's ranch in Colorado where we would also quail hunt and trout fish. Now how credible can you be as the President of Common CENTS Solutions telling employees that we have to tighten our budgets after spending a premium to fly cross country and spend several days at a luxury ranch? The second action was the contracting of a consulting firm (reference earlier metrics rant) half owned by Tenax. The expertise of these consultants was in government, not technology, and not only was their involvement a considerable waste of valuable time, their conclusions were truly bewildering. In the end their recommendation was to develop, with their help of course, an employee career path. We at that time were in survival mode trying not to impose layoffs, yet their priority was to implement employee career paths. Really? No, REALLY?

It wasn't too much later that I was in a critical board meeting with these Tenax venture company owners discussing the possibility of shutting down our company because the backlog had dissolved and we weren't generating enough new sales to replenish it. Of course, even then the greed factor remained. Our Tenax Company Board Chairman, the former CEO, suggested we downsize to just a skeleton support staff and continue to collect our substantial recurring revenues from customer subscription fees and reap the profits until it slowly faded away over time. If that kind of callous decision-making is what it takes to be wealthy, then I knew I would have to settle for something less. I argued that his suggestion was unfair to our customers since they were promised an evolving application and professional support for their subscriptions and without the capabilities of our R&D group, neither would be possible. And besides, I argued, no technician worth keeping would stay in such a dead-ended job. Therefore, the search for a white knight buyer began in earnest.

A couple of our larger competitors had expressed past interest in our company and much to my chagrin, now seemed the time to sincerely investigate their advances. However, we had a much better income statement and balance sheet at the time of their previous inquiries, so it was going to take a superior sales effort to convince them that we were experiencing only a temporary setback. Also changed from their initial approaches was the fact that each had been taken over by other venture capital firms.

So my first experience with a Venture Capital Firm was a sobering disappointment, one that almost put our company out of business. That led me to pursue the sale of our company to either of our two largest competitors. I first approached the friendliest of the duo, a company named Computrition, Inc. Computrition had solicited our sale consideration several years earlier when our financials were clearly in a more favorable position. Our venture partners asked a premium price that Computrition was unwilling to pay. Now however, it was questionable whether we could get even half our former asking price. To complicate matters more, Computrition, a former independently owned company, had itself been acquired by a large venture capital firm, Constellation Software, Inc.

As I mentioned previously, considering the circumstances, I regarded this as my most accomplished selling quest and it consummated in the sale of Common CENTS Solutions for 13 times its original value – not the return I might have dreamed of, but a reasonable return after 13 years in business. While we might have been acquired by Computrition, it became quickly apparent that Constellation Software was directing the decision-making. Having now relinquished all ownership, I agreed to continue as president along with my commitment that I could return the company to positive growth and profitability. Happily, I can report that when I left the company two years later, we were generating historic sales numbers and record profits. But it was a tenuous two-year relationship and a struggle of differing operating philosophies.

My aspiration for the sale to our competitor, Computrition, was to merge our product strengths for the mutual marketing benefit of both organizations. We were strong in the concept of "Lean" (a method of manufacturing inspired by Toyota to produce the greatest customer value with the least amount of waste in manpower and material) for meal production and delivery to hospital patients, but we were not as sophisticated with patient nutritional analysis. They were antiquated in their production model, but strong in diet management and nutritional analysis. We represented a comprehensive point-of-sale source and authored a proven cashless solution. They had neither, but possessed a base of large healthcare customers in need of these solutions. My expectation was that our companies would blend our strengths and each evolve into a more formidable force in our respective marketplaces. Through our synergies both our offerings would become more compelling. We could immediately expand our sales of POS systems and cashless apps; they could sell more of their diet and nutrition apps.

It seemed like a sure win / win situation. But that is not what transpired. I preferred to believe they naively dismissed the robustness of our applications, but regardless, they chose to ignore this working-together option.

Even at that, from my perspective, the relationship still looked promising. The venture company's initial prescription called for each company (Common CENTS Solutions, Computrition and a third smaller company purchased a year earlier) to operate independently and compete for business. Accordingly, they reasoned, by offering a client multiple independent options they increased the odds of a sale versus that other major competitor.   At first, we each operated autonomously, but when Common CENTS Solutions began to win business that Computrition forecasted, this internal strategy began to disintegrate. We had the more innovative solutions, the better cost/value proposition, and an appealing, altruistic mission. If this were the computer wars of the 80's, we were the DEC (Digital Equipment Corp.) minicomputer; they were the IBM mainframe. Like IBM, Computrition was focused on holding onto their legacy, high ticket systems, ignoring innovation, and like IBM they were vulnerable.

But back to my rant! Common CENTS Solutions had an altruistic mission, "Making life better for our customers and theirs" and it provided guidance for the conduct of our business. An honorable mission was something missing for this new venture. For them it was all about the money. Once they realized that we were a threat to their high margin Computrition systems, even though their systems were quickly turning into mainframe like dinosaurs, they began to disassemble our company, replacing competent experienced personnel with lower cost, entry level employees or not at all. Other seasoned employees were provoked into leaving for outside technology positions due to inane headcount reductions and cost of living wage freezes. And while we had a testing process to screen applicants for competency, this venture group had no formal vetting process. So, replacements were dubious at best. Mercifully for me, this all transpired after I retired.

Concurrently, while they were dumbing down the company's support, they were raising the costs to our customers. One of their first actions after my departure was to raise customer support fees by more than 30%. For me this was a distasteful action for several reasons:

1) As with any intricate application software system, the customer is a captive audience with little choice but to pay these support charges or risk a system failure without a lifeline. By contrast to their fee escalation, I always felt an obligation to be a good steward of our customers' support money. While we made a sensible profit from our support charges, we did so with only inflation matching annual increases and often with no increase at all. We kept our support charges contained with competent employees and creative use of technology. Besides, our real profits came from new and expanded sales and by managing support charges so adroitly, it became a marketing tool for acquiring new customers and retaining our longstanding faithful.

2) To justify their 30% increase they converted all customers to 24/7 maintenance, even though most customers had no need. How many hospitals have their cafeterias open or serve patient meals after 9PM? During my tenure we offered multiple support plans, including 24/7, for corresponding incremental charges, but it remained a customer's choice.

3) Although we kept our support charges reasonable, we had a metric to fix customer problems on their first call, not simply find a workaround and disregard the real cause. Our goal was to not have repeated customer calls for the same issue. In order to accomplish this goal it required top-notch personnel. As was pointed out previously, this venture company instigated unwarranted employee turnover then

restocked with mediocre replacements. I can only commiserate with my former customers for what is likely a high level of support frustration. And for this they were asked to pay a 30% premium!

Another of the venture company mysteries was their complete apathy for research and development. Before I left, our Common CENTS Solutions team strategically decided to aim our next generation of products toward cloud computing. Returning to the computer analogy we saw cloud computing applications as the PC replacing the minicomputer. Of course, after I retired our venture company parents decided to shut that development down. The return on our R&D effort was not soon enough for them. Imagine if that were the sentiment suggested to Apple, Inc. while they were developing their IPod or IPhone. We considered Common CENTS Solutions the Apple of our little niche world. So rather than a long-term strategy, they redirected the R&D efforts toward nebulous add-ons that "might" generate a fast buck.

Which brings me back to my initial aspiration to broker our POS solutions through Computrition. Turns out instead, the venture powers that be chose to develop their own POS solution because they thought they could make easy money from their loyal customers. Now recognize that we represented, as an authorized dealer, the world's largest hospitality POS solution, Micros Systems, Inc., with all the flexibility and capability their systems offered. Computrition spent months building their proprietary POS solution, which as I authored this chapter, had already undergone multiple rewrites. They wasted valuable R&D

opportunity developing an inferior "me too" application, rather than devoting their time toward a more constructive future product. Pity the poor Computrition customer that implements this albatross, for in a short amount of time they will realize their trust and monies were squandered. The obvious conclusion to be drawn from this POS episode is the crux of my rant about venture companies – GREED.

The following was the credo we lived by at Common CENTS Solutions while I was in charge.

Our Company's Vision is to provide:
   Customers with innovative solutions of tangible value in a trouble-free operating environment;
   Employees with meaningful work and business growth to allow them to reach their full potential; and
   Shareholders with profits attained through ethical business practices enough to perpetuate our vision and yield reasonable returns on their investment.

While these venture companies espoused that customers and employees were important, the reality of their actions showed that only profits were treasured. Every dictate and every action announced by the venture company "bosses" were aimed at squeezing more profit out of the system, mostly to the detriment of the customers and employees. Unfortunately, it appears that this short-term profit-taking is more universal than I might have realized. In a 2014 article in Time magazine, a survey of chief financial officers was referenced in which 78% indicated they would willingly harm their company to meet Wall Street quarterly financial targets. The article concludes that this thinking "will put American firms at a distinct disadvantage against global competitors with longer-term mindsets".

If I have one regret about my experience in starting and growing the Common CENTS Solutions business, it's that I wasn't able find the funding to acquire majority ownership when the parent company, Valley Services, made the decision to put our startup out for bid. I have zero regrets about what our company stood for, how we operated or how we treated our vendors, customers and employees. We had an altruistic mission and an honorable vision which guided us in all our actions.

At least that was true until we were overridden by the powers that be in these venture firms that held us captive to their greedy shortsighted views. They had only financial gain as their purpose and completely ignored our mission and vision. Certainly, this is not a unique occurrence when the company founder either abdicates or is stripped of his authority. Apple lost its way when they unseated Steve Jobs; Starbucks was in disarray until Howard Shultz regained its leadership. I didn't begin Common CENTS Solutions with the intent of gaining personal wealth, but it did provide me with a good living and an adequate retirement. And I sleep soundly every night with a clear conscience knowing I did my best to provide a valuable partnership for our clients and a constructive workplace for our staff. It is unfortunate that I couldn't obtain controlling interest to assure a company succession path that would uphold these values.

Returning to my TV show favorite, a member of the Shark Tank panel, Mark Cuban, summed up the essence of a good startup business: "find a problem and solve it, then work like hell to bring it to those that need it." There wasn't any mention of the money to be made. I firmly believe that the 'money making' model of the venture company, Constellation Software, is unsustainable and eventually its house of cards will collapse. Perhaps you can relate to my sentiments while reviewing the following summary of my venture firm takeover experiences:

· Dictatorial management structure. It's as if they hadn't read or didn't believe the research on management approaches espoused in tomes like 'Good to Great' (a statistical study on the commonalities of companies that have gone from good to among the very greatest and were able to sustain their positions over time). Before the venture firms we subscribed to the techniques of the self-disciplined, learning organization, whereas employees honor the mission, harmonize with policy, assume responsibility and share results. These venture firms had a top down management structure. They expected compliance rather than consensus.

· Autocratic decision-making process. Decisions for these venture firms emanated from their ivory tower HQ as if they were the only ones smart enough to make them. It became so petty that all new hires and pay increases had to have a corporate manager's permission, even though these were supposedly "independent" operating companies. After my departure they even instituted a policy that purchases over $100 had to have approval, including those made by our Sales VP and Chief Technology Officer (CTO). To say the least, employee morale suffered greatly from their lack of trust. In my world we planned our budgets annually and delegated the execution to the department heads, adjusting, if necessary, during the year for any unusual business conditions

· Managers, but no leaders. These venture firms placed good and loyal soldiers in management positions to ensure their corporate dictates were carried out without question. I was replaced by a part-time caretaker president whose qualifications were perhaps questionable. I say part-time because she resided 2,000 miles away where she was also the president of a declining company in the venture firm's portfolio. Eventually our VP of Sales, VP of Support and CTO were all replaced with only the CTO position filled by someone already within our organization. The replacements' pay was likely discounted and the individuals not always qualified or prepared for their positions. The entire structure was problematic because these new managers too often made decisions more for self-aggrandizement and recognition than for the organization's good. What kind of team spirit do you think this promoted?

· Cost of living raises; not competitive pay. During my final two years and for the couple after my departure, our particular company and the venture firm in general reported historic financial results. In fact, the venture firm's publications, both internal and external, boasted about the results. But when it came to administrating employee pay raises, the HQ "gurus" would only approve cost of living increases. Now understand that this was a period during which the US economy was recovering from the 'Great Recession'. The largest increase during this time was not but 2%. However, we were in the highly competitive software industry with a shortage of skilled technology workers, especially in our locale. We had some of the best technical knowledge workers, and as a result of this pay policy, we lost several. In comparison, before the venture firms, we each year conducted a competitive analysis in our region to assess the value of our employee base. As employees expanded their education and/or certifications and demonstrated their competence in new disciplines or responsibilities, we would seek to compensate them commensurately. While we never raised pay to the high end of the competitive wage / grade scale (we believed our culture offered a significant value), we did calculate what an employee's turnover would cost us, including loss of expertise, and issued raises accordingly. Any doubt that the venture firm's pay policy would force laudable employees to seek better opportunities? Of course they did.

· Corporate culture void. Like any of our admirable industry big brothers, think Google, Facebook, Apple, etc., we created a corporate culture of sharing, caring and fun. It was rooted in our mission and although we worked hard, we enjoyed it immensely. Our customer accolades were our rewards and made it all worthwhile. These venture firms never gave notice to our mission or our culture and I can't recall any stated mission of their own other than acquire businesses, squeeze out profits, and offload to a third party so venture shareholders make a bundle. Our culture of employee trust, responsibility and action was replaced by fear, discouragement and bureaucratic delay. Mindless headcount reductions, company reinvestments diverted to excessive profits, and corporate micromanagement created a cynical work environment in difference to our former supportive ethos.

· Metrics, metrics and more metrics. Previous chapters have well documented my sentiments on this subject, but rather than repeat my assessment of the venture firm's metrics ills, let me provide a different but recent example from a consumer's point of view. Let me also reiterate my awareness that metrics can be beneficial if they are well considered. The consumer in my example is me and it involves my lawn care service. I've used the same lawn service for many years and until recently have been generally pleased. But lately I've noticed a plethora of weeds in my yard unlike years past. While my front yard is weed-free, my side and back yards are overburdened. I was fortunate to arrive home a few weeks ago just as the service tech was finishing up a service on my yard. Curious, I questioned him on the demands of his job and learned that his lawn care company required him to service a number of homes each day, considerably more than he could fit into a normal 8 hours. THAT WAS THEIR METRIC. No wonder he attaches the report of service to the front door, rings the bell and takes off before the homeowner has a chance to answer. My guess also is that the tech sprays my front yard well (the company's public image) but quickly and haphazardly sprays my side and back yards to save time. Now I don't know what it cost them to acquire a new customer, but I do routinely receive from competitive lawn care companies, marketing materials through email and snail mail, as well as an occasional personal phone call or knock on the door. The acquisition cost must be significant enough.

And presently I am investigating those service alternatives with intent to switch. Would it not be better and more profitable for my lawn care company's metric to include monetizing quality (customer satisfaction) rather than just quantity (number of daily services)? This example is certainly analogous to several metrics the venture firms instituted at our company.

· Innovation a foreign concept. Prior to the Constellation Software venture company's takeover, we would withhold a percentage of our profits to invest in future innovations and improvements. This helped gain us a reputation as the most innovative company in our market realm. It allowed us to jump from DOS to browser-based, Internet like systems, skipping the problematic Windows versions. It allowed us to integrate hospitality concepts into institutional operations like cashless point-of-sale purchasing, patient room service, meal delivery dashboards and kitchen production displays. It allowed us to improve our support infrastructure and solidify our soaring customer loyalty ratings. After the takeover, R&D was confined to developing add-ons that might turn a quick buck with no view for the future. It became living for the moment and following the herd in place of innovate, invigorate and lead.

Less you now feel that all hope is lost there is some good news to buoy your outlook. To start there is a new and growing trend in corporate governance called the B Corp. As Time Magazine reports The B Corp, short for benefit corporation, puts employees, suppliers, the community and the environment on equal footing with owners and shareholders.

While profits still matter, it no longer dictates that investor returns must come first. B Corp is a new legal structure backing the concept of socially focused companies. There are currently more than 1200 certified B Corp entities, regulated in 26 U. S. states with legislation pending in 10 more. These B Corps are proving that you can be responsible and still make astounding profits and it's a fast growing phenomenon.

But the most heartwarming story I've read happened a few years ago. Here is the account from the newspaper article:

For those of us wondering how to explain that there is a difference between people and corporations and why that might matter, comes this summer's tale of the little grocery store that could. Market Basket, Inc. a 98 year-old grocery store chain with 71 stores throughout New England upended the story line about what it means to be a successful U. S. business.

Market Basket, Inc. was a successful corporation with an annual revenue of about $4.6 billion, that operated on the old-fashioned business model of low prices for consumers and high compensation for employees. Company CEO Arthur T. Demoulas offered not only profit-sharing bonuses to employees but also good wages, health insurance and pensions.

Unfortunately, Artie T., as his employees called him, was fired as CEO when cousin Arthur S. Demoulas managed to get control of the majority of the company's board and stock in July. Arthur S. Demoulas convinced enough board members that Artie T.'s approach was limiting Market Basket's profits – despite the billions in annual revenue.

Artie T. was replaced by two co-CEOs who immediately let it be known that the coddling of Market Basket employees was about to cease. When eight senior managers were fired for asking for the return of Artie T. and his pro-worker policies, Market Basket employees and customers began a five-week campaign to force the board to reverse its actions.

The new Market Basket board under the leadership of Arthur S. lost its case early in the court of public opinion, but it took the intervention of both the governors of Massachusetts and New Hampshire, as well as steep declines in company sales, before the Artie S. faction agreed to sell its 50.5 percent of stock to Artie T. and his allies.

Artie T. celebrated by telling Market Basket employees, "You have demonstrated to the world that it is a person's moral obligation and social responsibility to protect the culture which provides a honorable and dignified place in which to work."

When companies act more like faceless corporations than people working for a common goal, they tend to make decisions first and foremost based on the bottom line. As Artie T. might have said, "A corporation is not the same as a person, my friend". And so it is at Common CENTS Solutions since its takeover by those faceless venture capital corporations.

War Story #1 – Never Let Them See You Sweat

These next several stories consist of real life, actual events that occurred during my business career. Each has been chosen because they demonstrate principles espoused in previous chapters or are examples of the consequences when those principles are ignored. This first story is perhaps the most gratifying during our startup years at Common CENTS Solutions and it certainly validates the merits of good customer service:

Not long after Y2K, we were invited to submit a proposal to one of the USA's largest asset management firms for our point-of-sale and employee electronic payment systems. The invitation was proffered by their independent consultant who learned about our company through contact with several of our existing customers and heard their exceedingly positive feedback regarding our systems, service and support. This consultant's client, with managed assets in the billions, wanted to upgrade their food service outlets at their operation centers in New York, Denver and a newly built $300 million facility in Charlotte, moving from a peer to peer POS system to a client / server POS network.

Once the proposals were analyzed and pared down, we remained one of three finalists invited to their NYC headquarters to explain our attributes and exhibit our capabilities. We were each provided a tightly scheduled agenda that included a company overview presentation, a scripted POS (Point-Of-Sale) functionality demonstration, and a feature review and demo of software applications. These presentations were conducted consecutively over a two-day period, one after another.

As a general rule in competitive presentation situations like this, I always tried to be the last presenter. It afforded me the prospect of making the final, and hopefully lasting, impression. It also provided me the opportunity to refute or dispel any erroneous or misleading notions planted by the competition in their prior presentations. And in this particular case it offered me a unique advantage I hadn't ever anticipated.

At the time of this NYC presentation our two competitors were roughly 5 to 10 times our size with much deeper resources to devote to presales activities. We had neither the luxury of available staff nor surfeit finances to allocate to a non-revenue producing activity, and while we believed in our systems, and confident we had a reasonable chance to earn this client's business, we recognized the odds were certainly not in our favor. Therefore, it fell to me and our Chief Technology Officer to stitch together the most important presentation in our company's short history.

The scripted Point-Of-Sale part of the presentation included many intricate transactions and manipulations to show the power and sophistication of the offered POS solution. One of our competing vendors integrated the IBM system as their POS platform; the other, their then current vendor, utilized the Micros POS system. Of course, we too had adopted Micros as our POS standard. But the Micros client / server model was relatively new and not completely battle tested, and as was our practice we preferred to let others suffer the battle scars of early implementations and only subject our customers to installations of proven reliability. So here we were, the CTO and me, in our hotel room, past midnight the night before our presentation still trying to get the Micros POS system to perform several of these complex actions to no avail.

Finally, in the wee hours of the morning we decided to create a presentation plan B, knowing our credibility would be questioned when we couldn't perform some of the scripted POS routines. We did, however, have full confidence that if we did secure the business we could have the Micros POS system performing these routines and other gymnastics with ease. After all we had the highest proposal cost because we specified a powerful, high capacity server and enough implementation manpower to assure a smooth transition. For Plan B we decided to emphasize our strengths, which were our performance record and company reputation and our advanced, browser-based application software, and ignore, if possible, the POS activity. That meant expanding the overview portion of the presentation, skipping the POS script and demonstrating our state-of-the-art applications.
The next morning we put our plan into motion. I first gave the overview of our company, expanding its time by probing for comparisons to their current practices and issues. And it worked to perfection. Now considerably behind schedule as we came to the POS section of the presentation, my challenge went something like this: "Since we are behind schedule and you are all most interested in our new apps and how it fits into your future, and since Company X has already

demonstrated the Micros POS System capabilities, is there any reason to duplicate that exercise or would it be better to move forward and demonstrate your future?" The client readily agreed and with a deep inner sigh of relief I turned the program over to our CTO to demonstrate our advanced differentiated applications. To say the least, we left the presentation with the client in a high state of euphoria for our company and our systems.

We said our goodbyes and immediately thereafter the CTO and I headed to the nearest tavern, which we found overlooking Times Square, for the most refreshing and tasty mug of beer I have ever imbibed previously or since. Yes, we did secure this business; it was implemented seamlessly; and they remain a Common CENTS Solutions customer to the day this was written, 15 years later. It was by far our largest sale at that point, gave our company instant recognition and credibility, and acted as a springboard to our accelerated growth.

War Story #2 – Well We Called His Bluff, Didn't We?

As I mentioned in a previous chapter, I experienced my most difficult sales time during my tenure with the Burroughs Corporation in the '70s. While their mainframe computers were acclaimed for its innovative operating system and performance speed, over time their service record deteriorated to such an extent that retaining customers, much less capturing new ones, became an untenable challenge. This collapse was apparently the result of an ego driven CEO and his personal quest for a striking fiscal legacy.

In the beginning of this CEO's reign he was an astute executive, who during his early leadership produced a lengthy string of quarterly financial performances better than the quarters prior. But as the string stretched nearly a decade, instead of sound financial practices, he resorted to tricks and deceptions to keep the streak alive. It may have been the selloff of property and real estate, or cutbacks of inventory and service personnel, or the replacement of proven metal parts with unreliable plastic parts in the manufacturing process, or all of the above. It became his personal self-serving goal at the expense of an entire company. Apparently, he had an uninformed, passive Board of Directors to allow it to occur.

With that as a lead into this war story, my sales territory included several good Burroughs mainframe computer customers. In one quadrant of my geographical area, heavy in the manufacturing sector, I had two companies generating monthly revenue in excess of $75,000. Of course, IBM was the big blue monster back then and a formidable sales challenge in and of itself, so soliciting new customers required astute sales plans and good references. I was in the midst of an intense sales effort trying to convince a fairly large clock manufacturer to leave their long relationship with IBM and convert to our newest computer system. My primary contact was the Executive VP who was the son of the company's founder and who's last name was also the company's name. This period preceded the lowest depths of the Burroughs service problems, but they were already becoming serious. In fact, the endorsement from our most prestigious local customer was: "Our Burroughs computer may fail more often than our IBM did, but because of the multitasking operating system (in comparison to IBM's then sequential processing OS) we recover a whole lot faster".

We were down to the final decision meeting with the Executive VP and his evaluation team. They announced that they had decided to grant us the contract, but with a few caveats, the most pressing of which was computer up time. As the Executive VP put it: "If we ever have to run our programs at another site because of a computer failure, I will immediately cancel this contract and return to IBM, because we never before had to go off site". Well it wasn't too very long afterward that I was again face to face with the Executive VP, but now it's after his Data Processing team on 6 different occasions, had to pack up and travel 200 miles to a compatible backup site to run their systems. Having endured several previous gut-wrenching customer meetings alone and after pleading with the company to fix their faulty computer to no avail, I now had the Branch Manager with me and could only ask: "Rich (the Exec VP) what is it we can do at this point to make it right"? His reply with tears in his eyes: "Get it to work for one full week without a problem and I'll be happy". Can you imagine a grown man, an executive of a multi-million dollar corporation that bore his name, so distraught and frustrated with the computer that I sold him, that he had to fight to keep from weeping openly? I too, had tears.

As I told my Branch Manager on the ride back to the office: "From I'll cancel if it ever fails once to please have it work for one solid week" – "I guess we called his bluff". Yes, it was a sarcastic remark, but tinged in truth. And it was that day that I decided to make a change and never again find myself in a position where I would not have the authority to help my customers. It wasn't much longer that I accepted a position with the Food Service Contractor where I had more direct responsibility to assist customers. Oh yea, and Burroughs, they eventually lost all 3 of these customers and the $100,000 per month in revenue they represented. How dumb!

War Story #3 – Your Word Is Your Bond, If You Want Success.

I have talked before about how important reputation is to you and your company's business. It has a direct correlation to sales and profits. I relate here two compatible accounts. These war stories are examples of how a dependable, trustworthy reputation can advance opportunities for development and sales.

Not long after Common CENTS Solutions was acquired by our first Venture Firm (Tenax, Inc.), I had an appointment with a long-standing customer to invite them to buy our emergent patient room service application. This application was more concept than finished product with likely half a year's development work remaining before even a prototype could be delivered.

Because our venture partners were new to our software business, the owner's righthand man arranged to attend the sales call with me to learn more about our process. Aware that we didn't currently have a working program, no less an actual customer user, this executive asked: "How are you going to sell this system when you don't have any users?" My reply was basically a cocky "watch me". But what wasn't said and what he didn't understand was, as an established customer of many years, they had a track record with our company and because we had always followed-through on our commitments, they had a manifest trust in our promises.

So here we were in the meeting with several of the hospital's executives, including the food & nutrition director, and representatives from other pertinent departments. I presented the overview of our room service application and explained its current development status. Fortunately, our concept was well designed bringing innovation to the feeding of patients never before considered in the healthcare industry with many benefits for both the patients and the hospital. And this customer, a forward-thinking healthcare organization, loved the concept.

Despite the fact that we had no users, not only did this hospital customer sign up, they even offered onsite space and resources to our development team so we could expedite the project's completion. Totally amazed, my ride-along venture partner on the trip back could not stop talking about what he had witnessed. But really it all boiled down to one simple truth: say what you mean and mean what you say.

In the decade that this hospital had been our customer, we had always had an open dialog with truthful representations of our products. On those occasions when this customer requested modifications, we only promised what we could deliver and completed our commitments as promised. Building this level of trust and customer loyalty doesn't come easy but it certainly has its payback as this war story example points out so vividly.

My other example relates to our first restaurant hospitality customer after we took over the franchise for the Micros point-of-sale systems. Micros POS was an integral part of our solution for hospital and corporate retail food service outlets, primarily cafeterias. Because the then current Dealer in our locale was underperforming to Micros' standards, Micros approached our company requesting we become their dealer. Since it provided us dealer discounted pricing and direct communications within the Micros internal network, we agreed. But, of course, it came with responsibilities to sell and service local hospitality accounts.

Sales of Micros Systems to restaurants in our area were stagnant, so if we were to revitalize the market, we were going to need a new account with some prestige to add credibility to our dealership. Therefore, I targeted those better-known restaurants with a longstanding record for quality food and service. I found a celebrated Greek family restaurant in its third generation of ownership searching for a new point-of-sale system. During my survey I discovered that this restaurant had difficulty with their current POS provider (the dealer previously carrying the Micros line), particularly with an upgrade that took three database rewrites before it was suitable to operate. And of course, the downtime during these rewrites was not only an inconvenience, but a disruption of the business as well.

When we reached the negotiation stage for our Micros POS proposal, as any good restaurateur is prone to do, the owner pressured me for a discount, explaining that his current dealer always provided one. I explained that we priced our systems so that the margins produced could support the talent for the type of service and support the restaurant owner expected, and assured him he wouldn't experience the fits and disruptions of his past. He paid our undiscounted price; we lived up to our promise. As of this writing he remains a loyal Common CENTS Solutions customer, 16 years later, never regretting the trust and investment he consigned us. And this sale served as a springboard to the acquisition of many more restaurant customers going forward.

The message from these two chronicles is simple: TELL THEM WHAT YOU WILL DO, AND MAKE SURE YOU DO WHAT YOU TELL THEM. Your reputation and your future are at stake.

War Story #4 – What Is Your Business Purpose? Really? No, really?

As for having a mission, one particular experience sums up the power of a well-meaning business mission and purpose. This story was one I documented earlier, but I think it's so important that I am repeating it here.

We were proposing our patient room service solution to a sizeable healthcare organization in upstate New York. A large competitor had been working on this account for quite a while and had it listed on their sales forecast at a 90% probability to receive the order. We had performed our survey and documented our proposed solution and we now were in the homestretch reviewing the benefits of our proposal in a formal presentation to the Hospital's Administrators and all relevant Department Heads. During our presentation the Director of Information Technology, the competitor's advocate, vocalized objections to our proposed solution. He suggested the competitor's more expensive solution must be better. Then he followed-up with the blanket statement: "For all you software providers it's only about the money anyway".

Immediately I took exception to his statement, much to our salesman's trepidation, explaining that our mission – "Making life better for our customers and theirs" – is what drove our organization, from product development to sales and service, and if we remained true to that mission only then would the money follow. I explained that our mission statement wasn't just a slogan; it was a guiding principal for all our employees to ensue. And it was the performance benchmark by which we measured our company's success.

Because our mission statement was indeed sacrosanct within our organization, my passionate arguments apparently hit home with these hospital executives, perhaps even with the Director of IT. Needless to say, not long after the meeting we won the sale.

When an organization's focus is primarily financial ("it's only about the money") and the core to their decision-making, that organization is eventually doomed to failure. I've witnessed numerous examples from small startups to the largest of corporations. In fact, one instance occurred right here in my Mississippi neighborhood. Does anyone remember WorldCom? For a company to succeed it has to develop a mission that provides a meaningful purpose for its existence, one to which its employees can subscribe. Many of the most successful companies we're all familiar with didn't begin with the idea of making money. Instead they had missions of empowering their customers; i.e. personal computing, social networking, shopping from home, etc. Microsoft, Facebook and Amazon became behemoths of the industry because they kept their respective mission focus. IT IS NEVER ONLY ABOUT THE MONEY!

War Story #5 – Wisdom Can't Be Told!

When Common CENTS Solutions' majority ownership transferred from Valley Services to the venture firm, Tenax, the new company's executive committed to being a silent partner. However, as we built our installation backlog, due to accelerated sales, this executive could only see dollar signs and reneged on his commitment.

As explanation, the backlog consisted of contracted customers awaiting the installation of our systems, and it was after implementation that we collected the bulk of our revenue. But our systems required technician expertise to implement them successfully. As our sales growth outstripped our support staff, we would extend the installation schedule to allow time to hire, train and integrate additional technicians. That effort normally required six months to bring a new hire to competency.

But, when the supposed silent partner realized the extent of the backlog value, he naively usurped the process by hiring a technology challenged, financial friend with the charge to expedite implementations. As might be expected, installation quality suffered and sales waned. It was the classic Aesop's Fables goose that laid the golden egg. And of course, the executive absolved himself of any blame, instead pointing fingers at our staff.

The following is my letter to the executive board imploring them to reconsider their foolish path:

Guys,

Six-hour blocks of car travel to and from Nashville allows ample time to do some heavy thinking about the state of our company and consider all the conversations we've had in recent weeks. The one quandary I've heard time and again is: "how do we get our team engaged?" That question led me to contemplate the difference between now and two years ago when I felt CCS was performing at a high level of enthusiasm with a team looking toward the future and building the superior service reputation that gained the trust of the consultants and recently bore the fruit of the reemergence of Sodexho. By comparison, in the last two months one of us has either said directly or inferred that the following individuals should be asked to leave or outright fired – George, Ricky, Steve, Brian, AJ, Scooter, Dee, Darryll, and even Wolf. Most of these are the same teammates that were intrinsic to our early success and growth. If we've lost them perhaps it is us that should be fired. So, what happened?

Yes, I know your first response is: "but we weren't making money". Agreed, but it was also two years ago at about this same time that we all agreed the problem was top line sales. While we certainly thought we could be more efficient in our implementations, we had consensus that if the sales backlog were greater, we wouldn't have had so many vacant install weeks that eroded our profitability. Hence, we approved the investment to recruit a sales team. However, before we had the staff hired, trained, and productive we jumped the gun and brought in Jim to affect changes in the support area and the focus shifted from installation quality to installation quantity. In my opinion many of the customer service issues we are suffering today are the residual of that shift in focus. And in turn, these service issues had a demoralizing effect on staff attitudes. So how do we change it?

Certainly, we did learn better what our installation capacity is and that will help us going forward, but we applied the same single installer blueprint to all implementations when perhaps the newer GEMserve products required more. In fact, we ended up with multiple staff at each GEMserve site anyway, but only after the customers were totally disappointed and we had to make an all-out effort to salvage the installations. We need to think smarter and we need to entrust our staff to help us in that endeavor.

First, I propose we establish three unique teams with the mission to make quality yet profitable implementations in POS, GEMpay (including seniorGEM) and GEMserve. We would basically permit each team to chart their own success with our role only as advisor, one to a team. These teams would consist of members from both the Support and R&D Departments with the goals of better cooperation between departments, more efficient implementations and eventually zero installation defects. We would need a tracking mechanism to measure both customer satisfaction and profitability by project. We might consider as well a reward system to be shared by team members if goal thresholds are attained.

Secondly, we need to refocus on our mission "making life better for our customers and theirs" to give our staff a real sense of purpose and a performance benchmark that will empower us to beat our competition. At the same time we need to analyze our management style and I suggest we examine three concepts, Primal Leadership, Leading Geeks, and Good to Great, in that order and adopt or reject their principles, but end up with a blended style that brings clarity to the staff and eliminates the confusion that I feel strongly currently exists. I trust you have already read Good to Great, but I have copied sample excerpts from the other two to give you an insight into their fundamentals. We should set aside one hour weekly to discuss these principals and get to harmony as soon as possible. As with any discipline, I believe it is critically important to remain abreast of best practices. The best management styles of even ten years ago have been shown to be detrimental with today's employee generation. If we hope to successfully manage CCS, it is imperative we continue our education.

I look forward to meeting with you both to pursue this agenda and begin the reclamation of CCS' performance reputation. We really do have well intentioned employees and it would be shameful to release a third of our intellectual capital when with some creative management thinking we could reorient their attitudes to unleash their collective power. In a eulogy to Peter Drucker this week in USA TODAY it was said "His concepts turned companies away from treating employees as cogs, persuading management to think of workers as assets and partners, which is how the best companies behave today". If we are to treat our employees as true partners, we may have to abandon some present practices, but if we act quickly, I believe we can have the staff reenergized in three months time.

War Story #6 – Your Price Is Too High!

When we became an Authorized Dealer for the Micros Point-Of-Sale Systems, we accepted a responsibility to sell and service their systems in their Hospitality markets for our designated local territory, primarily restaurants.

Micros had little recognition in our market, so my challenge was to acquire a high-profile eatery that could jumpstart Micros' exposure. Afterall, Micros was the worldwide leader providing Hospitality POS systems. I targeted several locally owned restaurants with exalted reputations and approached each to tell the Micros and Common CENTS Solutions story.

One of my approaches was to a fabled family restaurant, named Primos. Primos restaurants had an outstanding reputation for its food and service.

Angelo "Pop" Primos, a Greek immigrant, opened their first restaurant in downtown Jackson, MS in 1930. The restaurant's legacy was passed down through the family, until the third generation had taken stewardship. Grandson, Don Primos, was the current owner of the then 3 restaurant chain.

I had noticed that on a recent visit for lunch, their POS registers were inoperable and the staff was in manual mode. As it turned out, their registers were newly installed, so my call was certainly timely. Long story short, Don was seriously considering our proposal to replace his still unpaid system. As it happened, the register system downtime I witnessed was just one of several in the few weeks Primos had been attempting to bring it online. Apparently, the selling POS dealer (who previously had the Micros line) had trouble stabilizing Primos' database and was in the process of re-establishing it for a third time.

We were in the final contract negotiating meeting when the inevitable comment surfaced. As all good Greek restaurateurs are apt to do, Don began asking for a better financial deal. Understand, as the premier POS system, Micros' suggested retail price was considerably greater than the alternatives. And my Common CENTS Solutions add-on expense for programming, installation and training, as well as annual maintenance, created a shocking cost escalation beyond Don's expectation. Considering his negotiated discounted price on the unsuccessful present system, it was quite a stunner.

Typically, this charge: "your price is too high". is the bane of many a salesperson, who upon hearing it, will immediately look for a price reduction. However, that was never my reaction. As I explained to Don he could opt for the lower priced system and suffer the continued business disruptions of system failures that not only cost him additional expense and peace of mind, but the possibility of lost business as inconvenienced customers abandon the restaurant. My proposition was for him to invest in our system and recoup many times the investment in the longevity of a capable and trouble-free operation. Further, I clarified that the price I proposed provided our company the proper margins to assure we could commit the resources to assure that stable operating environment.

Don did invest the full price of our proposal and I'm pleased to relate that Primos was a decade old, completely satisfied customer on the day I retired. Acquisition of the Primos account did accelerate our local hospitality sales and Common CENTS Solutions became a go-to source for restaurant POS systems.

War Story #7 – It's All Business

One of the more interesting prospective sales meetings I experienced was with the owners of the most popular New York City Gentlemen's Clubs, named "Scores". The owners' immediate needs were to better manage their clientele's spending and offer special privileges for their VIP guests. Longer term, the owners were on a mission of nationwide expansion.

Common CENTS Solutions was invited to participate in the business survey as part of the team with the Micros Sales Office for the metropolitan NYC area. Micros would control any of the cash or credit card transactions, while Common CENTS Solutions would offer a private VIP and guest debit/credit card as well as membership management all integrated with the Micros network.

To my surprise and contrary to my expectation, the meeting was not at the Gentlemen's Club, as might be portrayed on TV, but the Scores headquarter offices in a section of Manhattan, undergoing gentrification. The offices and staff were as professional as any corporation in which I had been involved. And the owners were all business.

A couple of the more fascinating findings during the survey phase of our sales campaign were:

1)   Our out-of-the-box CCS cashless card included a credit limit field of 5 digits, allowing up to $100,000 spending before suspension.

However, I discovered this was inadequate for their VIP members. While beyond my imagination, many Scores' patrons were multi-million-dollar contracted professionals – athletes, entertainers, Wall Street bankers, stockbrokers, corporate executives, etc. These big spenders could apparently exceed the $100 grand limit in just one night. And several did!

2)   Customers were not allowed to pay real dollars either for server tips or private dances or to throw on stage or place in the garters and brasiers of the dancers. I found that customers were required to buy "Scores Bucks", the equivalent of monopoly money. The method to this madness was that at the end of the night, the girls had to turn in their Scores Bucks in order to get back real money, allowing the company to capture their percentage of the tips and eliminate any skimming.

3)   In NYC, at least, the Scores Club was a fine dining restaurant and a destination for high level business transactions by members. Every aspect of the club was upscale, not at all seedy as might be the perception. I had belonged to a few private dining clubs in downtown Jackson, typically on the upper floors of our pseudo skyscrapers, but in no way so liberal or exclusive. Ours was dining only; Scores was dining with "bring on the dancing girls."

We were unsuccessful in our campaign as the Scores management chose a less expensive alternative, but I was happy to have been involved in the process, expanding my knowledge that a profitable business no matter its form, requires a well thought business strategy.

Fond Farewells

The following excerpts are from letters of goodbye that serve as good summations of my beliefs. The first was my retirement announcement to the Association for Healthcare Foodservice. The second was my final correspondence to the employees of Common CENTS Solutions.

To my colleagues and friends at AHF,

I send this communication to announce that after nearly 30 years in the Healthcare Food & Nutrition business, I will be retiring at the end of March. It has been my privilege to be associated with such an outstanding organization and an honor to have served on the Industry Advisory Council.

I have a pet quote from Albert Einstein that says: "try not to become a man of success, but rather try to become a man of value", and I have attempted in my personal and business lives to measure up to that creed. But it is also why my association with AHF has been so rewarding. Most every AHF member I have known has been a person intent on providing value to their respective organizations. We are all of a like kind – caring individuals more concerned with serving our customers, employees and peers than gaining personal recognition and treasure. In a world overburdened with greed, it is a comfort to realize there remains such good folk in leadership positions to set the example for our future generations.

I will still be attending the AHF National Education Conference in June and hope to see many of you there, but if I can be of help to anyone going forward, please feel free to contact me.

Tom Bunting

Dear CCS Staff,

To begin let me apologize for taking this long to thank you for the crawfish "roast" (and I thought it was going to be a boil) on Saint Paddy's Day, but I wanted to combine it with this one last communication to you. The roast was certainly a good time and your generous gift certificates were unexpected and typical of your penchant for going above and beyond. You really shouldn't have, but they are really appreciated as well. Thank you!

While many of you may have discovered new information, what with some of the war stories told, I too, learned something – that after many repetitions, we still haven't remembered the concept of CPTP. So, my parting message will concentrate on the history and meaning behind this forgotten concept.

When we first formed the company back in '98 we established 4 tenets that if we performed correspondingly would bring us success. I compared it to building a teepee that begins with 4 anchoring posts by which to construct the rest of the edifice. These tenets or anchoring posts are: Customer Service, Profitability, Teamwork and Personal Growth.

<u>Customers</u> are vitally important. Without customers we can't produce sufficient revenues to sustain the business. How well we service our customers determines whether they continue to buy from us and recommend us to their peers. Every business strategist agrees that for a company to thrive it must win the battle for customer

loyalty. And loyalty is won by providing real value, building a trusting relationship and never, ever taking customers for granted.

Profits are self-explanatory. It's what keeps us in business and provides the funds to reinvest in our future. To generate a healthy profit each employee has to frugally challenge their every expenditure and fairly bill for any rendered service. Customer loyalty will grow top line revenues and attention to cost and billing details will bolster bottom line profits – doing both simultaneously will exponentially amplify the results.

Teamwork is important on several levels. By cooperating with each other we can solve problems faster and work more efficiently, which has a positive impact on customer service and the bottom line.

Personal growth has the dual benefit of advancing the employee while it aids the company. Through cross-training and continuing education we learn new skills and acquire new information and thus become more valuable. And the company gains agility through expanded resources to tackle technical issues, make installations and backup sick or vacationing colleagues.

So **CPTP** are the four anchor posts that all employees need to embrace when they join Common CENTS Solutions. Once we embrace these tenets, we can build around them, acting accordingly to protect the company's wellbeing, and if we do that well enough we earn recognition for both ourselves and the company. This recognition over time becomes our reputation and the driver to transform quizzical prospects into loyal customers.

And so it happens this is also the blueprint for the construction of a teepee – four anchor posts surrounded by a protective cover and finally adorned with decoration. In the village that is Common CENTS Solutions each employee that joins the team, pitches their teepee and builds from there. My short slide show that depicts this scenario is attached for your amusement.

And finally, I must admit my retirement feels a little like being cast out of the village. I sincerely will miss you all. I respect and appreciate the contributions you have each made to position CCS for a wonderful future. But as I leave, I am rewarded by the glowing responses I am receiving from our customers, which lets me know we are on the right path. Perhaps Joanne Miller the F&N Director at Northwest Medical Center summed it up best when she replied: "Over the years I have had several dealings with your company and I would certainly say that you have proven to be a company of value. I wish all the vendors we deal with would follow your lead. Know that you have added a huge value to many food service operations." Do you reckon she will be buying from us again and recommending us to others?

Good fortune in the future. If you can remember CPTP, you can't miss.

Forever yours,
Tom

Final Thoughts

As my final thoughts for this CENTSable Startup manuscript I elected to summarize my philosophies and practices for running a business and living life. I couldn't however refrain from adding a personal opinion or two on current state of affairs that are irksome to me. I hope you agree.

Startup Priority – Develop a meaningful but brief mission statement and let it guide your actions from product development to sales to service. Hire smart and train employees on executing the mission, but recognize they may make mistakes before they 'get it'. Expect the best from your team and after training, delegate responsibility. If discipline is required relate it to how their action corrupted the mission. A phrase I used often was: "once is a mistake, twice is an image", and if they continue to fail, take prompt action, including dismissal. If they do well, pay them appropriately, but understand mission, training, responsibility and accountability will motivate better than pay.

Decision Making – Choose what's right. Don't be tempted by biased agendas. In my computer sales era, I had a large customer that was known to pray over difficult decisions. Obviously, this was quite a religious executive team, not unusual down here in the Bible Belt, but perhaps more fervent than most. While I never witnessed their actual process, it was told to me that the praying provided their answers. I do trust that whatever decision evolved it must have been a just one. That is my slant on decision making as well but without the religious aspect. While I was raised in a Christian environment, religion was not the force behind my decision making. I believe that decisions you make must be purely for the right reasons – not for personal gain, convenience or political favoritism. In today's climate this can be difficult. There could be pressure from greedy owners to choose profits over essential investments; it could be tempting as an ambitious manager to choose self-promotion over a proper course; or it could be easier to choose an expedient fix to avoid a more complicated real solution. I faced all these forces, but held true to my conviction and it served me and our company well. I can honestly say that my every decision was made without prejudice or a hidden agenda and always made with the best interest of our customers, employees and company's wellbeing in mind. I can tell you from my experience, making just and fair-minded decisions alleviates stress and promotes restful sleep, through both good and difficult times in the business. Nike has the slogan "Just Do It"; here it would translate to "Just Do It Right".

Work Attitude – There is much you can't control that affects your business and your life. To paraphrase a common saying: control what you can and don't fret over what you can't. But for sure there is one item you have total control over – your attitude. I've seen way too many managers with anger or complacency issues. You decide if you're going to bring a good attitude to each day......or not. Enthusiasm and a positive attitude are contagious and they are ingredients of leadership. One of my favorite quotes is from Lou Holtz, the former football coach. "Aptitude is what you're able to do, motivation is what you will do, and attitude is how well you'll do it."

Respect People – I believe everyone has something positive to offer, but perhaps not directly in your particular business. Everyone includes customers (even difficult ones), employees, vendors, peers, superiors, and even visitors. I mention visitors because I've had many salespeople call on me and I would always find time to meet with them, perhaps not always at that moment, but certainly later at a rescheduled date. This may be me paying it forward. I wrote in a previous chapter about my experience as a young salesman cold calling on executives. One was the President of a locally headquartered Insurance Company. Even though I had no appointment, this President invited me into his office to discuss my system with him. It had a profound effect on me, providing the confidence and encouragement to seek higher aspirations. A philosophy we had at Common CENTS Solutions was that everyone would leave better for having associated with us. We made life better for our customers, we treated our vendors fairly, and we revered our employees. We were proud of our minuscule customer attrition and employee turnover. We kept it serious but we also made it fun with success celebrations, customer appreciations, crawfish boils, pizza parties and the like. Yes, we had a business to run and sometimes had to release non-performing people, but we always gave them a fair explanation to help them on their way.

Continuous Learning – The world is moving at a breakneck pace and information changes at lightning speed. If you are to lead, you can't get complacent. You have to invest in continuous learning by staying inquisitive and curious. To keep abreast, read books, periodicals, and magazine articles related to leadership, management, your business, or operating practices. Take advantage of conferences, customer feedback, employee suggestions, and vendor and peer experiences. Be a good listener. Way too often I have seen individuals in leadership positions that somehow come to believe they know it all and have nothing more to learn. They skip out of conference sessions to play golf or engage in some other non-business related activity. They find excuses to not listen or ignore prudent advice. It's not too long after that they make ill informed decisions that are a detriment to the business and erodes their employees' confidence.

Health and Fitness – Starting and running a business, startup or otherwise, requires an extraordinary amount of energy. Believe it or not, you have to expend energy to create energy. The secret is exercise. Exercise, particularly the aerobic kind, keeps the body functioning properly and reduces stress and surprisingly produces greater energy to keep you going throughout the day. For several years as a former basketball player, I played in full court pick-up games at the YMCA after work. I never thought much about the exercise; it was just fun. But alas I got too old to remain competitive so had to find a suitable aerobic substitute. I really didn't care for jogging - too boring and too hard on arthritic knees, so I made a pact with myself. I would walk a mile and a half early each weekday morning only when it wasn't raining, fully expecting that would limit me to four days per week. Of course, as it happened, in my first six months it didn't rain at all at my 6:00 AM scheduled walk time. By then I had gotten into the routine, enjoyed the sunrises and clear morning air, and decided to expand to two miles on all seven days. I can say to get the most benefit your walk cannot be leisurely. It needs to be brisk at fifteen minutes a mile or better. At that pace you'll get your heart rate up and pump blood to all the vital organs, including the brain. But don't ignore resistance training and stretching as well. You don't need to be a body builder to engage in resistance training. I found more repetitions with slightly lighter weights is the way to go and most of my routine is using resistance machines rather than free weights. And keeping your core muscle groups strong through abdominal and back calisthenics will bode you well into your elder years. I also do believe you can improve balance and brain function by making use of both sides of your body. As a for instance, try brushing your teeth with your opposite hand or try turning your head in different directions, left and right, to breathe while swimming.

Diet and Nutrition – We all have heard the phrase "You are what you eat". I have thought I should write a diet book titled "Just Say No". I have been cursed through heredity with elevated cholesterol levels and although I was dedicated to my exercise routine, I had difficulty in controlling it. So, my next approach was to alter my diet. Starting in my late forties, each year I would say no to a food item or group in my diet that would have a harmful effect on my cholesterol and/or health in general. One year it was ice cream, finding frozen yogurt a good substitute. Another year it was butter. Soon it was high fat cheeses, fried foods, fast food hamburgers, and processed foods. In its place were non-fat dairy, baked, steamed or grilled vegetables, chicken, seafood and lean meats, natural salads with low fat dressings, and whole grain products. However, don't misinterpret, I didn't abstain completely from all those harmful foods. I would allow myself to indulge on occasion, but only sparingly. To my amazement I discovered that once I eliminated a food item, it wasn't long before I didn't miss it at all and sometimes even found it distasteful when next I dined on it.

Lifestyle – If you want to excel in your career or advance your company, you have to be prepared to perform at your peak. That entails living a healthy lifestyle among other factors. Everything in moderation is the proper mantra. Guard your eating and drinking habits. Control your portions and your consumption. Get a good night's sleep. You can't be at your peak performance hung over, bloated or overly tired. I looked at my job as I looked at my marriage. I had my wild and free time, but once I took on the responsibilities of marriage, I had to alter that lifestyle. So too, your lifestyle has to match the responsibilities of your business profession. Beside eating and drinking in moderation, you need to do it healthily as well. Opt for natural fruits, nuts and vegetables, whole grains and seafood. Make sure you consume the proper amount of hydrating liquids. I've been fortunate to have a position where I can afford fresh nutritious foods. When I think of all those less fortunate, I feel it would be negligent to not eat judiciously. I don't have to settle for fast food or low cost processed groceries. Nor, I bet, do you.

Technology – It is the year 2020 as I write this passage. I have witnessed the evolution of computer technology from mainframes to iPhones. I have seen, as well, the productivity improvements and information availability that technology has fostered. But today, I fear we have advanced perhaps a little too quickly, without the proper simplicities, safeguards and securities envisaged. In the age of mainframes, computers were designed to automate manual processes, like payroll processing or mathematical problem solving. Like my department store sale, they allowed electronic data capture and eliminated redundant manual data recording. For large organizations they were cost justified and enhanced their business operations. Next came mini-computers with a lower initial investment to reach smaller companies. They not only came with improved specific uses like accounting applications, but also offered generic programs like word processing. I can recall the productivity that word processing granted us in a function as simple as contract preparation. Beforehand contracts were prepared in multiple copies through a typewriter with carbon paper between the blank sheets. Make one typing mistake and you were starting over. However, the word processing program allowed you to correct any mistakes before printing the hard copies. Then capitalizing on those software foundations, came the desktop and portable personal computers that enabled individuals to work smarter and faster through use of spreadsheets and electronic mail. And these personal computers enabled the distribution of automation to remote operations. In my case we implemented desktop computers to Valley Services' far-flung contracted foodservice operations providing programs that improved their performance and productivity while automating the corporate data collection. However, before any program implementation, a thorough evaluation of user adaptability was scrutinized. For example, when we implemented automated timeclocks to manage labor, we had a choice of paper timecards with optical reading or the more advanced upcoming magstripe plastic cards. After analysis, we chose the paper timecards because it was a familiar process and many of our low wage employees at that time, were illiterate. These timecards could be marked or nicked so that those who couldn't read could still identify their individual cards. Simple!

But this was also the time that the dark side of automation began to surface in earnest. For awhile simplicity remained a theme for electronic devices. The Palm Pilot was an uncomplicated personal assistant; the iPod was a trouble-free way to listen to music; even the Blackberry was a simple, secure phone device. But then Silicone Valley chose to cram any and all functions into single devices, whether a laptop or an iPhone, making tech life more complicated and vulnerable. In the mainframe and minicomputer days, any theft or abuse was likely an inside job by an employee working for the firm. Now, with connections beyond the local users through networked servers, programs like email began to experience spam and hidden message malware. Today it's the age of the Internet Of Things and apparently all things hackable.

The push to advance technology was obviously done with little regard to the unsophistication of most end users or the possible incursion by the villainous and nefarious among us. I am somewhat cynical of today's tech world because of it. Even I, with a technology understanding, spend an inordinate amount of time troubleshooting and debugging my devices. My printer may be an all-in-one device for printing, scanning and faxing, but on the rare occasion when I needed to fax a document, the device didn't connect to my laptop and hence unplanned time to troubleshoot. Facebook likely had a worthwhile vision to bring people together, but never anticipated that it's platform would be used to disseminate false information that could sway a Presidential election or allow the criminal elements to recruit, scheme and publicize their dirty deeds. Phishing, identity theft, malware, data extortion and hacking are rampant in today's tech world. Is any of our technology safe? We've already seen hacker's home invasions through connected cameras. Will the mischievous be able to hack into self-driven automobiles and trucks and take over their control? How about terrorists or enemy states disrupting our air traffic or power grid, even downing planes or power? Yes, these days we are so engrossed with troubleshooting our complicated devices and protecting our precious information, that as much time is spent with these preoccupations as any productive endeavors. Sad!

Religion – Religion is one of those irksome items I mentioned at the start of this section. Let me first qualify that I am not anti-religion. I believe organized religions do many worthwhile projects to help the poor and downtrodden. But, for most businesses, it does not need to be brought into the workplace. At Common CENTS Solutions, our customers and potential customers were a diverse group of many different religious persuasions. A salesperson on our staff believed he had an obligation to spread the gospel according to his religious bent and I learned every correspondence he issued ended with a bible verse. It was inappropriate. His time spreading the gospel needed to take place on his personal time, not while conducting our company's business. If you have interest in my personal mindset on religion, I reference you to my autobiographical book titled "One Man's Unremarkable Life, Or Was It?".

Politics – Ah politics! If there is a more infuriating topic today, I can't imagine what it might be. Politics is the antithesis of all I have talked about in this book for building a successful company. In today's political environment there is no consensus mission, little, if any, teamwork and non-existent decision making for the common good. Today's politics is one of uncompromising positions creating stalemates and government shutdowns. Rather than looking for common ground and working together for the good of the nation, many members of Congress have taken a win/lose mentality in which the agenda is to block the other side from accomplishing anything worthwhile. And it has divided our populace into separate fanatical camps. Therefore, it is a topic to certainly avoid in the course of most any business, less you inadvertently alienate fellow employees and customers. Again, if you have interest on my political opinions, I reference you to my autobiographical book titled "One Man's Unremarkable Life, Or Was It?".

Thank you for your consideration of my viewpoints for starting and running a business. I trust it was interesting and hopefully enlightening. My intent was to turn what started as posts into an eBook to share these insights with anyone for whom it might have relevance.

Appendix

President's Annual Christmas Messages

For the last ten years during my tenure as President of Common CENTS
Solutions, I broadcast a message to employees at Christmastime intended
to both recap the recent year's happenings and offer food for thought. I
include it here because it provides a good chronological summary record
of the company's trials, tribulations, advances and successes from Y2K
until my retirement.

From: Tom Bunting
Sent: Tuesday, December 22, 2000
To: Staff
Subject From: : The President's Annual Christmas Message

CCS Team,

How the Grinch tried to steal Christmas:

I am sure the past few weeks have looked like the Grinch was trying to steal our Christmas, because we had several employees leave us to join other startup companies. While it is disappointing anytime turnover occurs, there is much to be cheerful about if we consider our opportunities. When people leave, it opens up positions so that our newer recruits can grow faster.

Here at Common CENTS Solutions, as you are aware, we select only the best of the talent regardless of the individual's experience, degrees or pedigrees. Often times it is a young talent looking for their first chance to break into the business. We have opened that door on several occasions. Sometimes it is an individual working in an entirely different line of business that is stymied in their growth and needing a new opportunity. We can look around us and acknowledge those folks in our organization. And many times, we interview individuals that, while in the technology field already, are frustrated by their working environment and seeking a positive change.

As I react to turnover, my first reaction is remorseful, but as we regroup, it has always proved to strengthen our organization. Pam has been promoted to Director of Administrative Support. Darryll has moved into the position of Director of Software Support. Ricky has progressed into Charge Posting support. Judy has taken over the leadership role on the POS installation team. Scooter has migrated to a position he coveted, the Help Desk Administrator. Craig has been hired as reinforcement to our hardware support. And Scott has come aboard to accelerate our sales growth. In each of these moves, our people have the immediate opportunity to demonstrate their value and to earn a commensurate reward in return.

But make no mistake – we have hired each of you because you are the best. Our testing proves you have the capacity to do well in our business and we intend to keep you with us. I will be working diligently to improve our working environment and the rewards for work well done. I will also be devoting my efforts to see that your loyalty pays at CCS, in the form of programs for longevity. We have a great beginning of a sound business for CCS. We have started up three years ago to evaluate if our model had potential. We have passed that benchmark with flying colors. CCS has been profitable for the second consecutive year in spite of paying for the investment in opening and selling without a devoted Sales Department. In other words, CCS has started its business the old fashion way, we have earned it. Unlike many of the startup companies these days that are flush with venture capital and spending willy-nilly until it runs out, CCS has built its business soundly without the indenture to the venture capitalists. Think of any successful company and the ones that have made it started the way CCS has. WorldCom, Skytel, even Microsoft all began with an idea and a shoestring. We have begun in kind and our prospectus is outstanding. How many of the Dot Coms are really doing well or will even survive this downturn? This year we will embark on a growth path that will move us to a new level of profitability three years from now. Those who help us get there will reap the rewards.

I WISH EACH OF YOU A VERY MERRY CHRISTMAS. I appreciate each and every one of you. Collectively, you are why the Grinch did not steal our Christmas. Have a safe and happy holiday and if our customers are covered, you may leave at 3:00 PM.

From: Tom Bunting
Sent: Tuesday, December 24, 2001
To: Staff
Subject: The President's Annual Christmas Message

Teammates,

Last year the hit movie was 'The Grinch That Stole Christmas', but this year, especially considering the events of September 11, it's all about giving. Certainly, it will be a positive outcome from the World Trade Center tragedy if we can put into perspective that life can be brief and the true joy in life is in the giving not the taking.

At this holiday time of year, we are reminded of the warm feeling we receive as a gift to a loved one is opened. We are also fortunate that the "gift" of service we render to our customers is valued by most. All year long as we surprise our customers with our touch of extraordinary attention, we should reap the same satisfaction from their grateful appreciation as we would when a friend cherishes a present. In return we receive their loyalty and endorsement that drives our company's growth and expands our individual opportunities for personal and professional progress.

While we may not always recognize or be recognized for the good we provide, it is proven through our records. We made the select list of the Forty Fastest Growing Companies in Mississippi in our first year of eligibility and I expect we will duplicate the honor in 2002. My joy is derived from the knowledge that as we continue to perform and thus grow, I can provide the rewards to help each of you attain your goals and reach your professional aspirations. So, thank you for your hard work this year. Keep it up! It's fun to work in a vibrant enterprise and serve a useful purpose.

I invite you to also consider serving others outside the confines of our company. Perhaps you might join a Civic Club, help build a Habitat for Humanity house, or donate your time to a worthy cause like Stewpot Services or Salvation Army. I promise you'll derive more benefit than you give and you'll gain a perspective for what is really important in life. I think it was Winston Churchill who offered the following quote and sums up my Christmas message: "You make a living from what you get; you make a life from what you give".

Have a safe and happy holiday. Enjoy the giving to your friends and family, continue to graciously give to our customers, and consider giving unselfishly to those less fortunate. Do and I'm sure you'll find that inner peace representative of this season. And as my gift to you, feel free to leave today after 1:00 PM, as long as your area is tidy and our customers are accommodated. Merry Christmas!

From: Tom Bunting
Sent: Tuesday, December 24, 2002
To: Staff
Subject: The President's Annual Sometimes Corny Christmas Message

Teammates,

In one of Tony Sopranos' therapy sessions this season, he came up with a profound observation: "Only in America do we think we're entitled to be happy". As I considered that statement, it brought into perspective how really fortunate we have it in America and here at Common CENTS Solutions. I think of all the world's people and how many are struggling to just stay alive, how many others exist in depressed economies and barely get by day to day, and even in the more advanced societies, the countless numbers that are stuck in mundane, dead ended jobs that pay only enough to afford the bare essentials.

Then I think of us at CCS. We have challenging jobs, the capability to earn a better than average wage, and meaningful work that makes life better for our customers, and in turn, for their customers. At this time of the year, it's important to not get caught up in the marketing hype of what we don't have – that designer label clothing piece, another jewelry trinket, the latest computer toy. Instead it's time to appreciate the many privileges that have been bestowed upon us. We each have unique talents, an environment in which to apply them, growth opportunities, and a happy workplace.

This past year has been our worst in terms of profitability, and although it was somewhat planned in our development and growth mode, it certainly is not a track we can continue for too long. However, it is exciting to consider the prospects for 2003. We have become expert in the Micros 3700 POS applications, we have integrated the Panasonic product line into our mix, and we have our new software products, GEMpay with all its modules and Gift GEM, out and stabilized. We penetrated the hospitality market last year and captured several "plum" restaurant customers and look to expand our base in the new year, we have begun to add Panasonic maintenance revenue at an increasing rate and see a large upside potential for its continuation, we have an installation backlog currently at $400,000 and have just finalized contract negotiations with two hospital systems for another $ 300,000, and we have begun preliminary talks with Wendy's International that could lead to a significant sale and a new vertical market.

As you can see, all the signs for a fantastic 2003 are positive, but it will require a total team effort to make it happen. We need to get a fast start by getting our backlog installed promptly and properly, we need to exude customer service that will build our premier reputation to attract more customers, and we need to be good stewards of the company's money by watching every penny of expense and collecting every charge due us. If we pull together as a cohesive team, we will see acceleration in our opportunities and secure our future. As I mentioned in the opening paragraph, in today's world, we are extremely fortunate to be in this position. I am depending on you to make us successful.

__I WISH EACH OF YOU A VERY MERRY CHRISTMAS__. I don't need to wish a
happy new year, because it is there for our taking. If our customers are serviced
and coverage for Christmas is arranged, you may leave after 1:00 PM. Be safe
and enjoy the holiday.

From: Tom Bunting
Sent: Tuesday, December 24, 2003
To: Staff
Subject: The President's Annual Christmas Message

Teammates,

Well we've come to the end of another year. And what an interesting year it
was! We announced new products for vending, gift cards and hospital room
service. We added the Sharp register line to accommodate our smaller
customers' need for a low-end POS device. We renewed our contract with our
largest customer, HealthTrust Purchasing Group. But most significantly, we
acquired new financial partners, J. L. Holloway and Max Bowman.
In reality, this is not just the end of another year, it is the beginning of a new and
exciting phase of Common CENTS Solutions' evolution. Our partners have seen
our potential and are investing in our success. We will be aggressively targeting
the marketplace, doubling our sales staff, working assigned territories and
vigorously promoting our products. This will translate into significant revenues
and profits. And we look at sharing some of that success with each of you. I will
unveil that program at our next staff meeting.

Of course, to attain our goals will take the dedication and undivided efforts of
each and every member of the CCS team. I know I can count on this team to
make it happen. I believe we are building something special here at Common
CENTS Solutions. I personally have experienced it twice before in my lifetime.
When the mission is honorable, the products sound and the team competent and

pulling together, there is not a more fun place to work. The work may seem overwhelming at times, but it certainly has its rewards.

I sense we are following our mission "making life better for our customers and theirs". I see it in the smile of our restaurant customers and the enthusiasm of our hospital clients. We not only provide a value to them, but our programs are satisfying the customers, employees and patients they serve. I invite you to continue to come together as a team, helping one another when asked and going the extra mile for our customers. It is our future.

As you listen to the music of this holiday season, I want you to think of the orchestra. Whether it's the Nutcracker or Handel's Messiah, think of the practice and cooperation that goes into making it a masterpiece. Each musician hones his/her skill so that the execution of the piece is harmonious and seamless. Each is focused on the overall satisfaction of the audience, with no one tooting their horn louder than another until the arrangement calls for it. Each perfecting their craft so that the movement is not corrupted with bad notes to the detriment of the listener's enjoyment.

We are the orchestra for the customers we serve and we need to learn the lessons of the symphony orchestra. Prepare yourselves for the installations to come. Learn our new products. Assist your fellow teammates. Be sensitive to the experience of our audience. If we do these things, I can perform my job like the conductor leads the orchestra, not with a big club, but rather a slender baton. When the team takes the responsibility upon themselves, I need only set the tempo and coordinate activities, just as the conductor does. It requires a team of professionals and I trust with a bit of polish we can be the premier "orchestra" in our industry.

If your work space is tidy and our customers are taken care of, you may leave at 2:00 PM today. Have a safe and happy holiday. Merry Christmas!

From: Tom Bunting
Sent: Tuesday, December 24, 2004
To: Staff
Subject: The President's Annual Sometimes Corny Christmas Message

CCS Team,

Let's suppose for a moment that Santa's sleigh is like an F-18 Fighter Jet. (It must be or how else could he make so many deliveries so fast?) As the pilot, Santa is flying over 700 miles per hour just 300 feet above the ground. He's tracking his destinations with his radar, he's communicating with his 7 elves (wingmen) on the radio, he's monitoring over 300 cockpit instruments -- all while he's sustaining nine bone-crushing Gs. And that's just for starters!

If he were a real Fighter Pilot, he'd have to takeoff, rendezvous with other aircraft, perform air-to-air refueling, engage enemy aircraft, deliver his ordinance and return to land on a moving aircraft carrier in the middle of the night -- all in one mission. So what is the secret that allows Fighter Pilots (and Santa) to fly such missions flawlessly?

Pilots follow a rigorous procedure called "The Flawless Execution Model" It's what precision flying groups like the Blue Angels use and it's a simple four step process that calls for Planning, Briefing, Executing, and Debriefing each mission to assure success every single time. And whether you're Santa, a Fighter Pilot or a member of the CCS team, the techniques of The Flawless Execution Model can dramatically enhance your performance. In a thumbnail here are the steps:

PLANNING - clearly defining the objective, identifying any potential threats, analyzing your strengths and weaknesses, rallying the support assets (teammates) from whom you need assistance, prioritizing your timelines, and envisioning the possible contingencies that might subvert the mission.

BRIEFING - a checkpoint meeting before the actual engagement which requires evaluating the plan with supervisors and teammates, agreeing on the tactics of who, what, when, where, why and how, documenting the agenda and preparing equipment and resources.

EXECUTING - carrying out the plan, occasionally referring to the documentation (checklists) when necessary to assure completion of key steps and procedures.

DEBRIEFING - the "no-fault" autopsy of the executed plan and how well it was performed, including the discovery of mistakes, the analysis of their root causes, the integration of lessons learned to affect a better outcome in future missions, and the dissemination of these new insights throughout the organization to eliminate error repetition and bring about an overall improved performance.

This is the secret to a Blue Angel performance and if we want to perform with the same precision for the profit of our company (and ourselves) we need to implement this form of disciplined management. We can only win in the long term if we plan carefully, brief our plan thoroughly, execute with discipline, and debrief so we can improve tomorrow.

In 2005, with our expanded sales team and great GEM products, you can expect that Common CENTS Solutions will be busier than ever. I have been promising to share rewards when we see it on the bottom line and I think 2005 will be the year we can all make it happen. But we will need to continue to work as a coherent team and begin to practice The Flawless Execution Model so as to not squander this opportunity.

Just as the Blue Angels became world famous or the Fulton Fish Market became world famous or even Santa, which began as a local story about St. Nicholas, became world famous, so too can Common CENTS Solutions become world famous. But we must plan our mission of "Flawless" Customer Service and execute it with the precision of these others.

Thank you for your hard work and dedicated efforts this year. HERE'S WISHING EACH AND EVERY ONE OF YOU A VERY MERRY CHRISTMAS. Enjoy the Holidays, recharge the internal batteries and get ready to hit the new year running -- the year when Common CENTS Solutions becomes world famous.

If your areas are tidy and our customers are taken care of (including assignment of the weekend support phones), I'm sure you will have little trouble convincing Jim to let us off early.

From: Tom Bunting
Sent: Friday, December 23, 2005
To: Staff
Subject: President's Annual Christmas Message

CCS Team,

It's been an exciting year! As you realize from all the new faces, we are growing quickly. And as we talked a year ago, we have shifted Common CENTS Solutions into a different gear, leaving behind the startup mode and accelerating into a real, maturing company. Over are the years of reinvesting potential profits to build the infrastructure and forward we move to a professional profitmaking entity. We have grown from 6 individuals when we started in 1998 to the almost 30 we now have. We have cracked the profit barrier this year and have been happy to share the rewards with each of you in a bonus check. And for 2006, if we each are mindful of our mission "Making life better for our customers and theirs" and do it in an efficient and economic way, we should see our revenues and profits soar. It will take dedication and a personal responsibility to look after the best interest of CCS and our customers, but I know it is within us.

We have had several sessions on "Leadership" in our staff meetings over the past few months, and I am asking each of you to find the leader inside. We need to not only grow our sales and profits, but we need to grow professionally as an organization as well. I am fortunate to have the opportunity periodically to attend conferences where new ideas on leadership and personal growth are explored. As I have in our staff meetings, I would like to share a few more with you in this message.

I heard an interesting session by the leadership coach for Yahoo, called the "Likeability Factor". As he stated likeability is an overlooked skill that can help you succeed in your career and in life. Your success does not only depend on the decisions you make for yourself, but more so, the decisions others make about you. Think about your job interview or a recent request you made for assistance. Your destiny was in how you presented yourself and really how the other person perceived you.

There is a psychological term called "Schema" that represents how humans feed on preconceived notions or prejudices to find negative judgment of others when often it doesn't exist. I am sure you dressed your best for your interview. Imagine if Santa wasn't shown wearing his red suit, but instead had on a pair of wrinkled jeans, shirt worn outside his pants and open toed shoes. Especially because of his age, beard and long hair most people would see him as just another homeless man. As we move to become more professional, keep this in mind and when visiting a customer imagine what their assessment of you must be. Believe me, that perception will have much to do with whether they take you and CCS serious or not.

Along the lines of likeability, we all enjoy individuals with good attitudes and high energy. Santa would not be very well liked if he wasn't jolly and enthusiastic and projected the high energy it takes to deliver toys around the world all in one night. Think about the image of Santa if he were constantly complaining the next time you want to moan about some extra work or a new reporting requirement as we learn to become a professional company.

And lastly, think about the likeable in the role models in your life. I bet they were individuals you saw as approachable and ones with whom you felt comfortable enough to share your thoughts. Again, go back to Santa when you were a child. He was there at the north pole (or in the mall) to hear what you had to say and understood what it was you wanted. Well, as the fellow from Yahoo summarized his message, it was - if you want to be liked in this world and get ahead, you need to learn it isn't about you, it's about the other person. The three most important traits you can develop to help you succeed are: 1) To listen. It is not just hear what's being said but actively listen to understand what's meant. 2) To empathize. Try to walk the mile in their shoes. And 3) Be real. (Where have we heard that before? Oh yea, the Fish video.) In other words, don't patronize. Be sincere.

We are fortunate to be in a thriving company with extraordinary growth, innovative purposeful products and now profitable. Of course, we have carved out our fortune by practicing as a company the Likeability Factor. For our customers our attitude is enthusiastic and our efforts tireless on their behalf. But most of all we have built our reputation on truly listening, empathizing and being real with them. In other words, Santa is much like Common CENTS Solutions. (Ok, the "real" part may not apply to Santa.)

I look forward to an exciting 2006 and the opportunity to work with each of you on a personal basis. I wish you and yours a Very Merry Christmas and a safe and happy holiday season. The attached is my Christmas card to you and your present, providing our customers are covered, is to leave any time after 2:00 PM today.

Thanking each of you for your contribution for our success.

From: Tom Bunting
Sent: Wednesday, December 20, 2006
To: Staff
Subject: President's Annual Christmas Message

Common CENTS Solutions Team,

Well here it is Christmastime again, the time of year when we should each gain some introspection and reflect on the many blessings bestowed upon us. It is also the end of the calendar year and another Common CENTS Solutions fiscal year. And what a challenging year it has been!

In the twelve months from August, 2005 through August, 2006 we've witnessed two waves of change wash over us here in Mississippi – one literal and the other figurative. Of course, we all know the trauma that the waves of Hurricane Katrina did to change our Gulf Coast and earlier this year most of us experienced the traumatic effect that change in an organization can bring. And change is what we had with the relocation of our offices, the institution and dissolution of the MICROS Healthcare venture, the engagement of the Capital Principals' consultant group, and the restructuring of our upper management team. Change is necessary for an organization to grow, but often it is difficult for individuals to accept and just like the coast residents during Hurricane Katrina, Common CENTS Solutions suffered its share of displacements. As a result, we've seen several good people leave our employ. But at the same time, we've seen many more employees embrace the challenge of change and dedicate themselves to seeing that our customers were unaffected by it.

Our always dependable "first responders" Ricky, Malcolm, Tony and George rolled up their sleeves and carried us through the difficult transition. Our newer employees Dee, Jacob and Benji proved their worth by absorbing the additional workload without complaint. Other departments willingly chipped in to cover our flanks and Russ, Richard and Lisa took on the dual role of support as well as development. Our ever steady and reliable Sales Director, Jim, continued to close sales while keeping our critical western regional customers pacified and happy. It is a tribute to these individuals that our customers remained unaware of the turmoil within and experienced only the same exceptional support and service that has become the trademark of Common CENTS Solutions.

Fortunately, we have replaced most of the abandoned positions with bright new talent and fresh insights. Clay has taken on the monumental task of learning our business while holding together three of our most demanding customer service areas - helpdesk, implementation scheduling and maintenance contracts. Linda and Jamie have come to the rescue of our administrative and accounting systems. Curt is unraveling the mysteries of our contracts and streamlining a process that had been wrought with inaccuracies. Brian has returned with his wealth of POS knowledge to give an instant boost to our support area, and Chris has arrived to provide an important technical bridge between R&D and Customer Support. Sales also received uplift with the hiring of Celeste and Bobby, both smart, young, aggressive and energized ambassadors for Common CENTS Solutions and certain to produce exponential dividends in time.

Like the mantra for the Gulf Coast residents: "what doesn't kill you will make you stronger", so too has the management team of Common CENTS Solutions become stronger. In the midst of chaos the management group of Max, Wolf, Scott, Linda, Clay, Ricky, Dee, Tony and me put aside any differences and perhaps worked more cooperatively than ever before. And like the Gulf Coast now that the surge has subsided, we can rethink our landscape and rebuild a better future. The first task at hand is to recover from our financial losses of this past year. Scott has agreed to take on the responsibility of leading the sales team. I have agreed to chip in and cover the vacant territories once handled by Eric and Mario. Max as CEO will be managing the day to day activities of the company and keeping our budgeting on track. Wolf will continue to bring to our markets innovative solutions that make our products saleable and keep us ahead of our competition. Linda will be watching our pennies, paying our bills and keeping us in good financial condition. And Clay, Ricky, Dee and Tony will continue to perform in their respective customer support responsibilities to assure that our reputation as a caring and responsive company continues to compliment our sales efforts.

And let's not forget the support of our financial partner, Tenax, and J L specifically. His willingness to not only endure the losses of 06, but continue to invest in our future is fueled by his enthusiasm for our potential and his vision for our greatness. J L has appraised many a different business opportunity and he knows a good one when he sees it. He is every bit assured that our company, Common CENTS Solutions, is money well invested. All we have to do is pull together and execute as the team Max alluded to in our staff meeting and we should see 2007 be a breakout year and a new beginning for us - just as the revitalization of the Coast after Katrina has already begun for them.

Yes, this has been a trying year for Common CENTS Solutions, but it pales in comparison to the trauma of those who suffered the direct impact from Hurricane Katrina. In keeping with that thought, I invite you here at Christmas to remember all those less fortunate and make a generous donation to the Salvation Army, Goodwill, Red Cross, your church or any charitable organization of your choosing. Better yet donate your time to Habitat for Humanity, Stewpot Ministries or other worthwhile endeavor to directly help someone(s) who likely in their lifetime will never have the advantages that you'll have in just this upcoming year. Certainly, it will put Christmas in its proper context and provide you a perspective for the great opportunity we have here at Common CENTS Solutions. Let's make it happen in 07.

Thank you for listening and... HAVE A SAFE AND JOYOUS CHRISTMAS AND A HAPPY NEW BEGINNING!

From: Tom Bunting
Sent: Tuesday, December 24, 2007
To: Staff
Subject: The President's Annual Christmas Message

The Common CENTS Solutions Team,

The theme of this year's message is "Loss and Gain". It certainly seems appropriate at this time of year when we all take time to reflect on our blessings and shortcomings. We are warmed by connections with friends and family at Christmastime, but we are also dampened by the recognition of personal imperfections in New Year's resolutions. We are joyous when we see children and adults enjoying the spirit of the season, but we are saddened when we realize many won't or can't be home for the holidays.

So too is it with Common CENTS Solutions. We suffered a bruising year in 06, but we delight in a remarkable recovery for 07. We have broken through that sales level barrier that, as our senior members recall, we always talked about getting past to put CCS on the path to predictable growth and profits. When the final financials are in, we will likely have achieved around $4.5 Million in revenue due to an ample backlog of newly sold customers and the dedication of the CCS Customer Support team to install it. Once we surpass the $325K monthly revenue mark our profits follow precipitously.

Our business has become successful more for the treatment of our customers than any other reason. Our unique brand of graciousness and responsiveness that only we know in the Hospitality State sets us apart and it's the legacy that must continue if we hope to thrive. We must remain true to our mission of "Making life better for our customers and theirs", and through this dedication we earn our customers' loyalty in return. Our customers will buy from us, stay with us and continue to recommend us. While we had our support failures this past year, we are committed to preventing those incidents in the next.

As for our team: It is a tribute to Scott and his sales team of old hand Jim, seasoned Bobby, and newcomers Ronnie and Tim that our pipeline of pending sales has never been better and our future never more encouraging. It is a comfort that our Research & Development team led by our CTO, Wolf, with his system experts Russ and Richard and documentation specialist Jim, provide us with the most creative, user friendly, results driven and stable applications in our industry. And our customers' compliments confirm that every day. It is notable that Clay has found his bearing and now has Customer Support poised for greatness. The contributions of George, Malcolm, Dee, Tony, Ricky and returnees Keith and Brian have never been more significant than in 2007. We look to these Customer Support stalwarts to provide our rudder as we navigate our future course. It is grand that Linda has our accounting processes well managed and Jamie has our Accounts Receivables, as well as some of us, under better command. Curt has worked hard to untangle the mysteries of our maintenance and support contracts and Celeste has applied her marketing talents to enhance our image at the helpdesk, on our website and in our marketing materials. And finally, we are grateful to have the backing of our Tenax partners Max and JL and the direction they have advised.

In other personnel matters we regret the year-end resignation of Ricky, but we rejoice in the return of Keith and Brian and the addition of the dynamic trio of Josh, Shanavia, and Charles. Staffing at Common CENTS Solutions is similar to the stock market. We make gains with additions like our trio and suffer losses like the departure of Ricky, but over time like the market we grow stronger and our worth steadfastly tracks upward. And that ascent will continue into next year. We have several unfilled new positions for which we are actively recruiting and plan for more as 08 progresses.

CCS has shown it's a terrific place to work, where if you have the initiative, a willingness to learn and an attitude to apply yourself, you can grow in your responsibility, professionalism and financial wellbeing. Ricky would be the first to testify to the CCS opportunity having come to the company eight years ago with lots of aptitude but little experience, yet through his resourcefulness he enriched his knowledge, became our application expert and support ambassador and nearly tripled his income. We are chagrin that we didn't have a commensurate position here to compete with the one for which he has been drafted, so instead we can only wish him well in his new endeavor. But that opens the door to the next rising Ricky(s) amongst us. It is a splendid opportunity for CCS staff to step forward and demonstrate their potential.

I close with a poem I heard a few weeks ago by Henry Wadsworth Longfellow titled "Loss and Gain":

When I compare
What I have lost with what I have gained,
What I have missed with what attained,
Little room do I find for pride.

I am aware
How many days have been idly spent;
How like an arrow the good intent
Has fallen short or been turned aside.

But who shall dare
To measure loss and gain in this wise?
Defeat may be victory in disguise;
The lowest ebb is the turn of the tide.

It's high tide now at Common CENTS Solutions and with your help we can ride the crest to a bigger and better future for all – you, our customer and our company. I anticipate a fun and fulfilling year and look forward to seeing us develop individually and collectively. HERE'S WISHING YOU AND YOURS A VERY MERRY CHRISTMAS AND HAPPY NEW YEAR!

Common CENTS®
Solutions

Dear Common CENTS Solutions Team,

Well here we are again at Christmas and the end of another year .... and indeed what a historic year it has been. We experienced the burst of the housing bubble and with it a collapse of financial markets not seen since the great depression eight decades ago. We've seen a year in which we had more serious presidential choices, including a woman, than ever before, which culminated in the election of our first African American President. We have likely been witness to the most consequential year in modern times.

Yet through it all, we at Common CENTS Solutions have seen steady sales, revenues and profits. And the 2009 forecast looks promising as well. Despite the setbacks in our 401K plans, we are fortunate that demand for our products and services remain high enough to not only retain full employment but perhaps expand next year. Count your blessings and be generous with your charitable gifts this year, because as of now two million other Americans have lost their jobs with many more pending.

Certainly, now is the time we look for leadership in our Federal Government to help us through this economic crisis and we all hope and trust President-elect Obama is up to the challenge. My guess from observing his actions thus far is that he is. That also is the subject of this year's message – Leadership. It is a quality that we all need to develop within ourselves and Common CENTS Solutions if we are to continue to prosper, especially through what is likely a difficult year ahead.

Mr. Obama has often invoked the memory of two of our greatest Presidents, Abraham Lincoln and Franklin Roosevelt when considering how he might lead. Abe Lincoln judiciously piloted America through its most fractious period of Civil War and FDR masterfully guided us out of our country's most devastating financial crisis, the Great Depression. The renowned historian, Doris Kearns Goodwin, recently wrote a synopsis on 10 leadership attributes that distinguished these two great presidents and they are lessons to which we should each subscribe.

1) **Courage to stay strong** – they had the talent to withstand adversity and stay self-motivated in the face of frustration.

2) **Self- confidence** – they surrounded themselves with people of diverse perspectives that could disagree without fear of retaliation.

3) **Ability to acknowledge misjudgments** – they were willing to admit and learn from their mistakes.

4) **Amenable to change** – as conditions changed, they adapted and responded.

5) **Emotional intelligence** – they encouraged advisers to give their best and remain loyal.

6) **Self-control** – they managed their emotions and kept calm in the midst of trouble.

7) **Popular touch** – they had an intuitive awareness of public sentiment and a sense of when to be tolerant and when to be assertive.

8) **Moral compass** – they had the courage and integrity to follow their convictions even when they risked losing popular support.

9) **Capacity to relax** – they understood the value of temporary getaways to return to their duties with revived energy and clear headedness.

10) **Gift to inspire others** – they had the ability to communicate their goals and educate the people, thereby shaping public opinion.

As we head into 2009, we will each need to practice these traits. I suspect our customers will not be as fortunate as we and will be accepting greater workloads with fewer employees. Locally, we have seen several Healthcare organizations announce employee downsizings and no doubt it is even more severe in other parts of the US. But this is where Common CENTS Solutions can help, and if done right, cement ourselves as the premier solution provider. We've got to stay motivated. We have to work as a team. We need to learn from our mistakes. We have to be extra careful with our spending. We have to stick to our mission's moral compass – "making life better for our customers and theirs". And we have to communicate, communicate and communicate with our customers.

If we do these things we will become a true leader in our industry and while our competitors struggle we can flourish. We will see many changes in the coming months in USA global relationships, the national economy and I expect even our company. Those who learn to be leaders will position themselves to move ahead, while those who linger in old habits will be left behind. As always, but especially through this period of economic recovery, customer service needs to remain our priority. Now is our opportunity to seize the initiative and build our reputation for responsive, dependable service. In the end, it will be this reputation that secures future sales in better financial times.

This Christmas, let us all be most generous with our prayers, money and time, because so many people need them. Let's pray that Barack Obama has the gifts to be the right leader for our country. Let's pray that those who have lost their jobs, houses and wellbeing recover quickly. Let's share our good fortune through donations and volunteerism to help others who are especially hurting. And let us each commit to being the best individuals we can be.

Here's wishing you and yours a Safe and Happy Holidays and a Prosperous New Year!

Dear Common CENTS Solutions Team,

The days sure go by quickly when you're busy! And busy we've been the last half of 2009. It seems like only yesterday that I was sending out last year's Christmas message. For this message it is with my sincerest gratitude that I thank each and every one of you for your dedicated and diligent efforts in making this a truly successful year for Common CENTS Solutions. We have seen profits while other companies have gone bankrupt. We have experienced stability while other enterprises have had massive layoffs. It is a tribute to the CCS Team that we continue to thrive in the harshest of economic times.

We had a new beginning in 2009 with the acquisition of Common CENTS Solutions by Computrition, Inc. and its corporate sponsor Constellation Software, Inc. The strength and compatibility of being with a sister company dedicated to Healthcare Foodservice and a parent corporation exclusively made up of software companies, puts us on a path of dynamic growth for our venture and advancement for our employees. With our new culture we can again return to the Common CENTS Solutions' Vision to provide:

Customers with innovative solutions of tangible value in a trouble-free operating environment;
Employees with meaningful work and growth to allow them to reach their full potential; and
Profits, through ethical business practices, enough to perpetuate this strategy and produce reasonable returns for shareholders.

To fulfill our vision for our customers, it will take us all working together. To generate the profits we envision, it will take maximizing our billings and minimizing our expenses. And to empower you, our employees, it will require a steady stream of new business challenges, as well as increased opportunities for self-learning. I especially look forward to providing you access to learning experiences this year that will broaden your knowledge and add to your skills. But it all starts with you.

The Holiday Season is a good time for reflection and in that light I share with you an article I recently encountered. This excerpt relates to the subject of personal development discussed in the editorial:

Six Sets of Questions to Ask Yourself (if you dare)!
By Chuck Sink

These six principles and sets of *questions* could have a high impact on your life and business performance. Dare you ask these questions of yourself?

1. Do you have the capacity to be completely honest with yourself? If you don't, you're doomed. Can you think about your own thinking and recognize when you are rationalizing your behavior rather than being an unbiased referee of your motives? The whole truth will set you free to accomplish your noblest goals!

2. Acceptance of people, places and things as they are, not as you would have them, opens deeper understanding of how the world works. Acceptance is not advocacy or approval. Do other people and situations disturb you often? Do you fret about injustice, politics, culture shift or coworkers? Temporary, justifiable anger is understandable and acceptable but holding grudges or harboring resentments is not. Remaining angry at a competitor, customer, supplier or anyone else is bad business. You can't change them but they sure are affecting your thoughts and attitudes, aren't they? Don't let them.

3. Script and build better character traits based on service to others instead of self-enrichment. Is your character based on how good you look or how good you are? Can you believe that serving others is the only way to serve your own best interests?

4. Know what you're great at! Do you recognize what your unique, best-in-class talent is? What do you love to do? What tickles your creative imagination? About what do people compliment you the most? That is probably your key to a rich and happy life!

5. Get excited about what you know you can accomplish and apply the necessary discipline to keep yourself accountable. Can you pull away from distractions and apply yourself to important work? Can you tell yourself the truth about whether you're procrastinating or moving ahead? You've got to get excited enough to look forward to working. It's called work for a reason but it will be fun if it's what you're best at!

6. Allow self-fulfilling momentum to kick in and turn a labor of love into labor you love. The brass ring of career success is looking forward to Mondays. Do you love your job? Is your work exciting, fulfilling and fun? Are you serving and making your customers better off?

Any roadmap for success in business begins with an introspective analysis of yourself and what personal traits hold you back from accomplishing your fullest potential. What was your reaction to these six sets of questions? There is no better Christmas gift I can give each of you than the opportunity for personal education and training to increase your value to our company, to our customers, but above all, to yourselves. And that is what we intend for 2010. Make good use of it.

So again, thank you for a great finish to 2009. Let's keep that momentum going into the New Year. As I always do, I remind you to think of the less fortunate at this time of year. Nothing puts life more clearly in perspective than serving the downtrodden in a soup kitchen or on a Habitat house. So, donate generously, especially your time, to your favorite charity and the biggest surprise of all will be the pure joy you will reap in return. It's like the same joy that children get when they discover on Christmas morning that Santa has been there.

Here's wishing you and yours a Safe and Happy Holidays and a Prosperous New Year!

Common CENTS®
Solutions

Dear Common CENTS Solutions Team,

Well here we are again at Christmas and in a tradition that's been going on for a decade, my message for the season. Because I'm getting older and approaching retirement, this could be my last. As we end 2010, I am rewarded both by how we performed as a company and for how we are positioned going forward into the next decade.

As we stand now, because of an avalanche of year end orders, our bookings (sales) should exceed our goal set back in January. Despite a disappointing first quarter, the pace of our installs picked up and remained steady throughout the other three and we now should be close to meeting our 2010 revenue and profit metrics. Our cash generation has never been better – $1.7M better than 09 – and our backlog starting the New Year should be near record levels. And speaking of the New Year, we will see a brand new website that will enhance the image of Common CENTS Solutions and augment our ability to capture more sales. It is through all of us working together as a team that has pulled us through and put us in this winning posture.

Pulling together as a team reminds me of a leadership book I've read in recent weeks. The book title is "Iditarod Leadership" and as the name implies, it is the story of a consultant that goes on an introspective, self-improvement quest disguised as a school to learn what it takes to lead a dogsled through the tough and frigid Alaskan wilderness. The external lesson learned was that it takes a good team of individuals placed in the right positions, cared for and rewarded, before they will pull together and put your sled in a winning position. In his case it was obviously a dog team, but the translation to any work team was unavoidable. But the larger lesson was more personal and he was forced to look inside himself for the characteristics that produce a real leader – one that can direct any team to victory.

Along with this book, I also read a recent article in a Sales publication that told the story of an underprivileged boy who never received any wished for gifts from his Christmas list because his family was too poor. As the story was told this boy grew up to become a very successful salesman and one day right before Christmas he decided to become his own Santa Clause and rewarded himself with the gifts that he could never afford as a boy. Well combining these two stories, my message this year is for you to become your own Santa and reward yourself the gift of self-improvement as was learned by the Iditarod participant. This year give yourself the gift of:

ü Optimism. A positive attitude will always carry you regardless of how dire the circumstance appears. It's easy to fall into a "Grinch" mode when there seem to be more service requests than time available, but if we attack those times with a positive zeal, it's amazing how quickly the problems subside. After all, you are performing a valuable service and making life better for many patients, food service workers, retail customers and the owners or executives of the organizations you serve. Knowing that should be a reward in and of itself.
ü Learning. You are in an enviable position, because you have a job that provides you the chance to continuously grow your knowledge base. It's a job that continues to provide challenges and allows you to utilize your wit and skill and intellectual talent to solve them. Take advantage of these learning opportunities.
ü Persistence. Never give up, never give in. That is certainly the slogan for those who enter the Iditarod race and one lesson the consultant learned. Only the tough minded and persistent become leaders.
ü Wisdom. Understanding that you don't have all the answers takes insight and accepting advice from others can save many hardships in the long run. Seek and accept the wisdom from your leaders and peers.
ü Sacrifice. No pain, no gain. You have to put in the time and sweat equity if you want to advance in the business world and it will take some sacrifice if you want to improve yourself and your lot in life.
ü Gratitude. If you ever want to shuck off the blues, just write down a list of the things you are thankful for. You have meaningful work with good personal earnings potential, you have job security as your company came through the

Great Recession unscathed, you provide important services to those who entrust you and you are valued by your company leaders and peers.

ü Service. Sir Winston Churchill once said "You make a living from what you take, but you make a life from what you give." How true! You have plenty of opportunity to give service to our customers, but you should also consider those less fortunate than you in the community. Donate to your favorite charity. Give of your time to help someone in need. It is actually the best Christmas gift your can give yourself because the sense of pride from giving service will bring true joy to your heart.

I thank you for your contributions to Common CENTS Solutions' success this year. I wish you all a Safe and Happy Holiday and look forward to seeing you in the New Year.

Common CENTS Solutions

COMMON CENTS® SOLUTIONS

Our Mission is to provide:

- Our customers with innovative solutions of tangible value in a trouble-free operating environment;

- Our employees with meaningful work and growth to allow them to reach their full potential; and

- Profits through ethical business practices, enough to perpetuate our strategy and produce reasonable returns for shareholders.

Inside:

Microsoft CERTIFIED Partner

A Message from the President.....

Every member of the Common CENTS Solutions' team enjoys an employee friendly environment that offers fun yet challenging work. It is important to us that our team members have the opportunity to balance work with their personal life. While we work hard and, on occasion, long hours we believe in compensating by providing the benefits of flex-time scheduling, paid-time-off, and a sincere concern for each and every one of our employee's personal and professional well being.

At Common CENTS Solutions, we emphasize teamwork, and our mission for customer satisfaction will always take precedence over individual agendas. This does not mean individual growth is not a priority. We pride ourselves on fostering an atmosphere of opportunity for individual achievement and professional growth.

Tom Bunting, Preside

Common CENTS Solutions remains competitive in the job market with base compensation supplemented by liberal incentive and reimbursement programs. However, our greatest reward is not monetary but special recognition from our clients for a job well done.

I am looking forward to your contributions continuing our company's drive for leadership in our industry. It is my sincerest desire that your assignment with Common CENTS Solutions will prove to be a rewarding and enriching experience.

-Tom

Our Technology

At Common CENTS Solutions, we are committed to developing and marketing quality state-of-the-art software products for the food service industry. Our flagship product, GEM, is designed and developed using the latest Microsoft® server technology, giving our clients a highly desirable web-enabled browser interface. We deploy our solution on the best of the POS platforms, and we are an authorized dealer for MICROS and Panasonic, the world leaders in hospitality POS systems.

Work Environment

At Common CENTS Solutions, we combine time-honored traditional values with a high-tech software and consulting firm to create a work environment that is unlike any in the industry. Our success depends on a caring and sensible staff that places a collective priority on developing solutions to meet client needs. As a result, we have earned and are proud of our strong reputation for extraordinary client satisfaction.

Jim and Pam discussing a sales contract.

Although we are a professional firm that emphasizes teamwork above all else, we provide opportunities that enable our team members to tap into their full individual potential.

Many high-tech hardware and software firms expect team members to obligate themselves to their work sacrificing quality of life with family and friends. It is our belief that to be more successful in life one must strike a balance between work and personal freedom. At Common CENTS Solutions, we are committed to a business casual atmosphere promoting a reasonable work schedule as the norm rather the abnormal.

Our staff is rewarded with generous paid time off, benefits plan, and educational assistance for those who desire to continue their learning.

Our Medical Benefits

Our team members are offered enrollment in quality, comprehensive medical and dental programs as well as a short-term and long-term disability plan. The benefits don't end there! We offer additional pre-tax offerings such as accident, vision, hospital and major medical supplements, including cancer coverage.

Informal meeting in Tom's office.

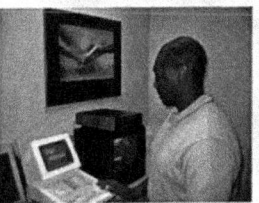
Tony testing a POS machine.

Our Savings Benefits

To help our staff build a strong, stable financial future, we offer a generous 401(k) Retirement Plan. Our plan is pre-tax including a matching plan by the company. Many members of our staff appreciate the ability to change their 401(k) elections as often as they like by using an automated telephone system. We provide a *free* Group Life Insurance Plan and a Voluntary Term Life Plan.

You can also take advantage of our Members Exchange Credit Union that provides competitive savings and loan alternatives that tend to be more appealing than those offered by many financial institutions.

Compensation

Our compensation plan is very competitive in the marketplace. There is an attractive commission schedule for our sales team and the implementation teams are eligible for a bonus program that is not deferred compensation. All of our staff members are eligible for special bonus programs during various projects for demonstrating exceptional service.

In keeping with our commitment to quality of life, travel schedules are not excessively demanding and are intermittently spaced. An exciting incentive we offer our traveling team members is all frequent flyer mileage points and hotel points earned are yours to keep and use as you desire! Many companies require the program points to be used for *business purposes only* but this is not so with Common CENTS Solutions.

If you travel for Common CENTS Solutions, you are issued a corporate credit card and calling card. You are allowed to call home once each day using the calling card while traveling on company business. Another creative travel incentive is the travel per diem plan. Each day while on the road you are given a generous tax-free per diem. Any unused per diem is yours to keep. In addition, some companies require employees to share hotel rooms. We respect your privacy, and do not follow this common practice!

Steve prepares for a client implementation.

Paid Time Off

We have an attractive sick pay and holiday schedule designed to help you balance work and family life. Our sick pay benefit allows an employee to accrue up to eight weeks of paid leave, a valuable benefit for those unexpected or extended illnesses.

Whether you plan a cruise, a European vacation, or a long weekend retreat in the mountains or to the beach, our newest staff members do not have to wait a full year to make their vacation a reality. Our team members begin accruing vacation time from date of hire up to eighty hours within the first year. Accrued hours can be taken *after only six months of employment*. Our tenure-based vacation plan allows staff to earn up to five weeks of vacation.

Richard answers a customer's question.

Life @ Common CENTS Solutions

Our management team believes that it is important for all staff to be well informed about the company direction and status. To help meet this very important function, we have regularly scheduled staff meetings and periodic updates. On the lighter side, we enjoy an occasional pizza party and host an annual holiday social that includes your spouse or significant other.

The Team discusses a process.

201

Common CENTS Solutions

Success Tenets

The Seepe Teepee
C P T P

 Common CENTS Solutions

Success Tenets

It takes a village to build a company
Employees take up residence in the village
And set up their teepees

Anchor by four supporting posts
Fashion exterior around them
Decorate & improve the shelter

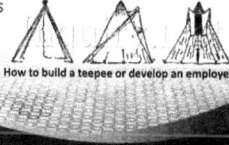

How to build a teepee or develop an employee

 Common CENTS Solutions

Success Tenets

Our Four Employee Anchor Posts

Customer service
Profitability
Teamwork
Personal growth

Save Shorty

When Common CENTS Solutions was first spun off from our Mothership, Valley Services, the six employees that transferred with that endeavor had to be reoriented from a previously bureaucratic large organization to a nimble startup company. I needed a mission that sent a clear message to these six teammates for what was most important. At the same time I had to represent that the new environment was not going to be the stuffy, regimented corporate world, but more a fun, high energy setting. Hence, I devised the simple, cartoonish mission, easy to recall and meaningful in its intent. It was a name twist from a popular movie of that time, "Get Shorty", which also helped keep our mission top of mind.

As we progressed through the years, I would often refer back to this mission to make the customer service point. The following memo was issued around seven years into our startup and after we had already updated our mission to the more altruistic "Making life better for our customers and theirs". It is followed by the cartoon representation for "Save Shorty". Bet you can't dismiss the image from your memory once you've seen it!

Common CENTS Solutions Team,

I have been made aware that my email on the above subject may have been misinterpreted and this email will hopefully clarify the matter.

When I choose the subject of "Customer Service" it represented for me the global term for what our entire company is all about; it was not intended to single out or demean a particular department within CCS. It is the mission of each and every one of us to "make life better for our customers......" and we are all equally responsible for that. To twist a phrase from the founder of Starbucks Coffee, Howard Schultz, "we are not in the software business serving customers; we are in the customer business serving software".

I believe it is important to share with you what our customers are saying so that we all can be mindful of our company's perception and benchmark what we do well and what we need to improve upon. This began on our very first day as Common CENTS Solutions back in 1998. Back then our mission was a simple "Save Shorty" (a sequel to a movie released in the prior year) where Shorty was the Food & Nutrition Director short on time, money and resources and our charge was to save the day by removing the burden of the POS from his/her many tasks. Concurrent with that mission, we held monthly get-togethers with a Shorty Says segment to share what we had heard from our Shorty(s) – both good and bad.

The success of CCS is truly a team effort. If Sales doesn't know our products well enough to configure properly and/or set a realistic expectation, if R&D doesn't design and code stable programs or willingly collaborate when unsolved problems escalate, if Customer Support doesn't provide solid installs or offer timely, effective solutions to helpdesk calls; if Administration doesn't prepare contracts and invoices promptly or accurately, and if Management doesn't listen and act on the customer and staff suggestions, then we will not reach the level of success for which we strive.

The fact that one department felt ostracized by my comments tells me we are not working as a unified team. Customer Support has the most difficult and contentious job to perform – caught among what R&D has enabled the program to do, what the sales person has committed it will do, what the customer expects it to do and what the program actually does do. And to top it off, management anticipates it will always be a favorable outcome. Believe me, sometimes that is a no-win situation.

Each of us at Common CENTS Solutions need to be cognizant of the important role that Customer Support performs for us. While we can hold frank discussions in search of ways to improve, we will not tolerate the blame game. Next time something doesn't go according to plan, don't point fingers. Instead ask what you personally can do to help..........and don't be surprised to discover it may be you that created the problem in the first place!

Tom Bunting

"Save Shorty" - Common CENTS Solutions Mission 1998